D0058164

BOOKS BY CALVIN TRILLIN

UNCIVIL LIBERTIES

FLOATER

ALICE, LET'S EAT

RUNESTRUCK

AMERICAN FRIED

U.S. JOURNAL

BARNETT FRUMMER IS AN
UNBLOOMED FLOWER

AN EDUCATION IN GEORGIA

THIRD HELPINGS

THIRD HELPINGS

CALVIN TRILLIN

TICKNOR & FIELDS

NEW HAVEN AND NEW YORK

1983

Library of Congress Cataloging in Publication Data

Trillin, Calvin.
Third helpings.
1. Food—Anecdotes, facetiae, satire, etc.
2. Cookery—Anecdotes, facetiae, satire, etc.
3. Gastronomy—Anecdotes, facetiae, satire, etc.
I.   Title.
TX357.T7   1983   641.3'00207   82–19517
ISBN 0–89919–173–8

Printed in the United States of America

S 10 9 8 7 6 5 4 3 2 1

Portions of chapters 6 and 11 originally appeared,
in different form, in *Travel & Leisure* and a portion of
chapter 1 originally appeared in the *Nation*. Portions of the
remaining chapters first appeared in the *New Yorker*.

To Alice and Abigail
and Sarah — the same old crowd.

Contents

Spaghetti Carbonara Day

I HAVE BEEN CAMPAIGNING to have the national Thanksgiving dish changed from turkey to spaghetti carbonara. In a complicated way, it all has to do with my wife, Alice. There came a time when Alice began to refer to a certain sort of people I have corresponded with over the years — the sort of people who are particularly intense about, say, seeking out the best burrito in East Los Angeles — as "food crazies." She spoke of them as bad company. She even spoke, I regret to say, as if I might be in danger of becoming a food crazy myself. I knew I had to do something. What I decided to do was launch a campaign to have the national Thanksgiving dish changed from turkey to spaghetti carbonara.

At one time, Alice had displayed a certain sympathy for my approach to eating. Maybe "understanding" would be a better word. When I began traveling around the country in the line of duty some years ago, she understood that if I didn't devote a certain amount of my time to searching out something decent to eat I would find myself having dinner in those motel restaurants that all buy ingredients from the same Styrofoam outlet or in that universal Chamber of Commerce favorite that I began referring to as La Maison de la Casa House, Continental Cuisine. That is not a fate to wish on a husband simply because he may have an irritating habit or two — insignificant ones, really, like a tendency to eat from the serving bowl late in the meal.

When did it all begin to change? The signs, I now realize, were there almost from the start. Why, I should have asked myself, do dinner-table conversations at our house so often turn to the perils of gluttony? Why had Alice continued to preach the benefits of limiting our family to three meals a day even after I presented incontrovertible scientific evidence that entire herds of cattle owe their health to steady grazing? Why, in planning a trip to Sicily, would Alice seem so insistent on staying in towns that have world-renowned ruins, whether those towns are known for their pasta con sarde or not? Looking back, I realize that I shouldn't have been so surprised on that dark and rainy night — we had just arrived in a strange town after a long trip, and I was inspecting the Yellow Pages in the hope of happening upon some clue as to where a legitimate purveyor of barbecue might be found — when Alice uttered those dreaded words: "Why don't we just eat in the hotel?"

Naturally, I tried to put everything in context.

Around that time, I happened to read in the *Dallas Morning News* that a Frenchman who goes by the name of Monsieur Mangetout had been hired to entertain at a Dallas waterbed show and had done so by eating several cocktail glasses, a few dozen razor blades, and about a third of a queen-size waterbed, including the pine footboard with brass brackets.

"Now that is excessive," I said to Alice. "The article says that he once consumed fifteen pounds of bicycle in twelve days, and he's negotiating with Japan to eat a helicopter."

The point I was trying to make to Alice — who, I must say, was not really keeping up her end of the conversation — was that compared to somebody like M. Mangetout (who, I hasten to admit, is obviously on one extreme), I am someone of moderate appetite. When M. Mangetout talks about eating junk, after all, he is not talking about those packages of roasted sweet-corn kernels from Cedar Rapids that I love. He is talking about eating junk. Just as an example, I have never eaten so much as a pound of bicycle. Although Alice may criticize me for always showing my appreciation of the hostess's cooking by having a second helping — to be perfectly honest, what she criticizes me for is showing my appreciation of the hostess's cooking by having a third helping — I can see myself acting with considerable restraint at a dinner party at which the main course is, say, queen-size waterbed ("No thank you. It was delicious, but I couldn't eat another bite"), even though I might risk spending a sleepless night from worry over the hostess's feelings or from the effects of the first helping.

The comparison I drew between me and M. Mange-tout did not impress Alice. I began to see that the problem was not context but point of view. Seen from the right point of view, for instance, someone who seems intent on obtaining a fair sampling of foodstuffs wherever he happens to be is engaged in serious research — not research done for the purpose of, say, probing for soft spots in the New England fast-food taco market, but the sort of pure research that in more cultivated times was often done by educated gentlemen interested in knowledge for its own sake — and the appropriate way to comment on such research would not be with phrases like "You're making an absolute pig of yourself."

What better way to demonstrate one's seriousness than to start a campaign to change the national Thanksgiving dish from turkey to spaghetti carbonara? Alice would see some serious historical research going on, right under her own roof. Our daughters might be convinced that my interest in food is far too complicated to be summed up with the phrase "Daddy likes to pig out." They are always being told that an informed citizenry is the cornerstone of democracy, after all, so they could appreciate the value of informing the citizenry that the appropriate Thanksgiving dish is spaghetti carbonara. The adventure inherent in such a campaign might even stir their souls sufficiently to free them from what I regard as a crippling dependence on canned tuna fish.

It does not require much historical research to uncover the fact that nobody knows if the Pilgrims really ate turkey at the first Thanksgiving dinner. The only thing we know for sure about what the Pilgrims ate is that it couldn't have tasted very good. Even today, well-brought-up English girls are taught by their mothers to boil all veggies for at least a month and a half, just in case one of the dinner guests turns up without his teeth. Alice and I did have a fine meal of allegedly English food in New York once, at the home of a friend named Jane Garmey — it included dishes with those quaint names the English give food in lieu of seasoning, like Aunt Becky's Kneecap — but I suspected that Jane had simply given real food English names, the way someone might fit out a Rumanian with a regimental blazer and call him Nigel. I liked the meal well enough to refrain from making any of the remarks about English cooking that I often find myself making when in the presence of our cousins across the sea ("It's certainly unfair to say that the English lack both a cuisine and a sense of humor: their cooking is a joke in itself"), but I can't get over the suspicion that hidden away somewhere in the Garmey household is a French cookbook that has a recipe for something called *La Rotule de Tante Becky*.

It would also not require much digging to discover that Christopher Columbus, the man who may have brought linguine with clam sauce to this continent, was from Genoa, and obviously would have sooner acknowledged that the world was shaped like an isosceles triangle than to have eaten the sort of things that English Puritans ate. Righting an ancient wrong against Columbus, a great man who certainly did not come all this way only to have a city in Ohio named after him, would be a serious historical contribution. Also, I happen to love spaghetti carbonara.

ॐ

I realize that these days someone attempting to impress his own wife and children with his seriousness might be considered about as quaint as Aunt Becky's kneecap. Where we live, in New York City, just having a wife and children is considered a bit quaint. I sometimes think that some day we might be put on the Grayline Tour of Greenwich Village as a nuclear family. As I imagine it, the tour bus pulls up to the curb in front of our house, after the usual stops have been made at Washington Square Arch and Aaron Burr's stable and Edna St. Vincent Millay's brownstone and Stephen Crane's rent-controlled floor-through. As the tourists file out, a fat lady in the back of the bus says, "How about the hippies? I want to see the hippies." Instead, they see us — an American family. Mommy and Daddy and their two children are having dinner. Mommy asks Abigail what she did in school all day, and Abigail describes a math problem that Daddy doesn't understand. Mommy is helping Sarah cut her meat. Mommy is telling Abigail to sit up straight. Daddy is telling Sarah that if she doesn't stop playing with her meat he will arrange to have her sent to a foster home. Mommy is discussing the perils of gluttony. Daddy is being manipulated by Abigail and Sarah, who want a cat. Mommy says Daddy hates cats. Daddy says it's not that he hates cats — Daddy doesn't want to teach Abigail and Sarah prejudice — but simply that he has never met a cat he liked. Mommy is helping Daddy cut his meat. After a while, the tourists seem to grow restless. The sight did seem unique at first, but it has begun to remind them of reruns of the old "Ozzie and Harriet" show. The tour guide, discerning their mood, leads them out the door. The fat lady says, "Now can we see the hippies?"

The tourists might assume that such a family celebrates Thanksgiving every year with a traditional meal at that same dinner table. Not so. When it comes to national holidays, there is a quiet war for hearts and minds going on in our family — it is fought over Halloween and Christmas — and Thanksgiving has tended to get overlooked as territory that is not hotly contested by either side. Halloween is my holiday. For days before Halloween, people who telephone me have to be told by Alice, "He's in the basement making sure that the witch piñata is still in good enough shape to hang out the window" or, "He's upstairs trying to decide whether the ax-murderer's mask goes better with his Panama or his Stewart Granger bush hat." I'm always in town for Halloween. Even if I didn't happen to enjoy walking in the Village Halloween parade in my ax-murderer's mask, I would feel it my duty to be there because of the long-established role of a father in passing on important cultural traditions to the next generation. Alice's attitude toward Halloween, I regret to say, borders on the blasé. By the time Halloween comes, Alice is already thinking about Christmas, a holiday whose modern celebration always makes me wonder whether December might be a nice month to spend in Saudi Arabia. As a result, we engage in one of those quiet struggles common to marriages of mixed cultural emphasis. If I were not in town to press my case on Halloween, I sometimes think, my girls might find themselves spending October 31 trimming a Christmas tree — pausing now and then to hand out tiny "Joyeux Noël" wreaths to the visiting trick-or-treaters.

Being a kind of demilitarized zone, Thanksgiving has often been celebrated away from home. It was at other people's Thanksgiving tables that I first began to articulate my spaghetti carbonara campaign — although, since we were usually served turkey, I naturally did not mention that the campaign had been inspired partly by my belief that turkey is basically something college dormitories use to punish students for hanging around on Sunday. I did bring up some esthetic advantages of replacing turkey with spaghetti carbonara — the fact, for instance, that the President would not be photographed every year receiving a large platter of spaghetti carbonara from the Eastern Association of Spaghetti Carbonara Growers. (As King Vittorio Emmanuel may have said to his Chancellor of the Exchequer, spaghetti doesn't grow on trees.) I spoke of my interest in seeing what those masters of the floatmaker's art at Macy's might come up with as a 300-square-foot depiction of a plate of spaghetti carbonara. I reminded everyone how refreshing it would be to hear sports announcers call some annual tussle the Spaghetti Carbonara Day Classic.

I even had a ready answer to the occasional turkey fancier at those meals who would insist that spaghetti carbonara was almost certainly not what our forebears ate at the first Thanksgiving dinner. As it happens, one of the things I give thanks for every year is that those people in the Plymouth Colony were not my forebears. Who wants forebears who put people in the stocks for playing the harpsichord on the Sabbath or having an innocent little game of pinch and giggle? In fact, ever since it became fashionable to dwell on the atrocities committed throughout American history — ever since, that is, we entered what the intellectuals call the Era of Year-Round Yom Kippur — I have been more and more grateful that none of my forebears got near this place before 1906. When it comes to slavery and massacring Indians and the slaughter of the American buffalo and even the assorted scandals of the Spanish-American War, my family's hands are clean. It used to be that an American who wanted to put on airs made claims about how long his family has been here. Now the only people left for our family to envy are the immigrants who arrived in the last decade or so. They don't even have to feel guilty about the Vietnam War.

Finally, there came a year when nobody invited us to Thanksgiving dinner. Alice's theory was that the word had got around town that I always made a pest out of myself berating the hostess for serving turkey instead of spaghetti carbonara — although I pointed out that even if a hostess had taken some offense at the mention of my campaign, she must have forgotten all about it in the glow of hearing me ask for thirds on stuffing. Abigail and Sarah, I'm happy to say, did not believe that our lack of invitations had anything at all to do with my insistence on bringing the spaghetti carbonara issue to the attention of the American people at any appropriate opportunity. They seemed to believe that it might have had something to do with my tendency to spill cranberry sauce on my tie.

However it came about, I was delighted at the opportunity we had been given to practice what I had been preaching — to sit down to a Thanksgiving dinner of spaghetti carbonara. In the long run, I saw it as an opportunity to inspire our daughters to seek the truth and test frontiers and engage in pure research and never settle for eating in the hotel. In the short run, I saw it as an opportunity to persuade Sarah to taste spaghetti carbonara. Sarah does not taste casually. Abigail has expanded her repertoire to the point of joining us in the ritual lobster supper we always have in Maine on the way to Nova Scotia, where we live in the summer, but Sarah celebrates that occasion each year with a tuna-fish sandwich. ("The tuna fish here is excellent," she always says.) If Sarah is finally persuaded to try something new, she usually cuts off the sort of portion I have come to think of as a microbite, chews on it tentatively, swallows it, and says, "It's OK, but I'm not crazy about it."

Confident that our family was about to break new ground, I began preparations for Thanksgiving. I did some research on what ingredients would be needed for the main course. I prepared for any questions the girls might have about our forebears:

"Was Uncle Benny responsible for the First World War just because he was already in St. Joe then?" Abigail might ask.

"Not directly," I would say. "He didn't have his citizenship."

"Is it really true that your grandparents got mixed up about American holidays when they first got to Kansas City, and used to have a big turkey dinner on the Fourth of July and shoot fireworks off in Swope Park on Thanksgiving?" Sarah might ask.

"At least they had nothing to do with snookering the Indians out of Massachusetts," I would be able to say. "Be thankful for that."

Naturally, the entire family went over to Raffetto's pasta store on Houston Street to see the spaghetti cut. I got the cheese at Joe's Dairy, on Sullivan, a place that would have made Columbus feel right at home — there are plenty of Genoese on Sullivan; no Pilgrims — and then headed for the pork store on Carmine Street for the bacon and ham. Alice made the spaghetti carbonara. It was perfection. I love spaghetti carbonara. Sarah, a devotee of spaghetti with tomato sauce, said, "I'm not crazy about it," but she said it in a nice, celebratory kind of way. After a few forkfuls, we paused to give thanks that we weren't eating turkey. Then, I began to tell the children the story of the first Thanksgiving:

In England, a long time ago, there were people called Pilgrims who were very strict about making sure everyone observed the Sabbath and cooked food without any flavor and that sort of thing, and they decided to go to America, where they could enjoy Freedom to Nag. The other people in England said, "Glad to see the back of them." In America, the Pilgrims tried farming, but they couldn't get much done because they were always putting their best farmers in the stocks for crimes like Suspicion of Cheerfulness. The Indians took pity on the Pilgrims, and helped them with their farming, even though the Indians thought the Pilgrims were about as much fun as teenage circumcision. The Pilgrims were so grateful that at the end of their first year in America they invited the Indians over for a Thanksgiving meal. The Indians, having had some experience with Pilgrim cuisine during the year, took the precaution of taking along one dish of their own. They brought a dish that their ancestors had learned many generations before from none other than Christopher Columbus, who was known to the Indians as "the big Italian fellow." The dish was spaghetti carbonara — made with pancetta bacon and fontina and the best imported prosciutto. The Pilgrims hated it. They said it was "heretically tasty" and "the work of the devil" and "the sort of thing foreigners eat." The Indians were so disgusted that on the way back to their village after dinner one of them made a remark about the Pilgrims that was repeated down through the years and unfortunately caused confusion among historians about the first Thanksgiving meal. He said, "What a bunch of turkeys!"

As is traditional after a Thanksgiving family meal, I was content. I considered the campaign a success even if no other family converted. Everything seemed possible. I could see the possibility of doing pure research (not "pigging out") around the country in the company of like-minded researchers (not "food crazies"). I could see the possibility of inspiring Sarah to try dishes far more exotic than spaghetti carbonara. I could see the possibility of Alice's thinking that someone given to serious inquiry might have a third helping out of an honest curiosity about whether it could taste even better than the second. I had a third helping of spaghetti carbonara.

An Attempt to Compile a Short History of the Buffalo Chicken Wing

I DID NOT TRULY APPRECIATE the difficulties historians must face regularly in the course of their research until I began trying to compile a short history of the Buffalo chicken wing. Since Buffalo chicken wings were invented in the recent past, I had figured that I would have an easy task compared to, say, medievalists whose specialty requires them to poke around in thirteenth-century Spain and is not even edible. Alice, I must say, was unenthusiastic about the project from the start. It may be that she thought my interest in pure research could lead me into searching out the origins of just about any local specialty I might contemplate eating too much of — how the cheesesteak got to Philadelphia, for instance, or why Tucson

is the center of interest in a Mexican dish called
chimichanga, or how people in Saginaw came to begin
eating chopped-peanuts-and-mayonnaise sandwiches,
or why a restaurant I once visited in the market area
of Pittsburgh serves sandwiches and french fries with
the french fries inside the sandwiches. I assured her
that I had no intention of extending my inquiries as far
as chopped peanuts or interior french fries, although I
couldn't fail to point out that she had, in a manner of
speaking, expressed some curiosity about the Pittsburgh
sandwich herself ("Why in the world would anybody
do such a thing?").

I saw the history of the Buffalo chicken wing as
a straightforward exercise, unencumbered by the
scrambled folk myth that by now must be part of the
trimmings of something like the Philadelphia cheese-
steak. There happens to be extant documentation
identifying the inventor of Buffalo chicken wings as
the late Frank Bellissimo, who was the founder of
the Anchor Bar, on Main Street — the form of the
documentation being an official proclamation from the
City of Buffalo declaring July 29, 1977, Chicken Wing
Day. ("WHEREAS, the success of Mr. Bellissimo's tasty
experiment in 1964 has grown to the point where thousands of pounds of chicken wings are consumed by
Buffalonians in restaurants and taverns throughout our
city each week . . .") I would not even have to rummage
through some dusty archive for the document; the
Anchor Bar has a copy of it laminated on the back of
the dinner menu.

I had the further advantage of having access to what people in the history game call "contemporary observers" — a crowd of serious chicken-wing eaters right on the scene. A college friend of mine, Leonard Katz, happens to be a Buffalonian — a native Buffalonian, in fact, who became a dean at the medical school of the State University of New York at Buffalo. I have also known his wife, Judy, since long before the invention of the chicken wing. She is not a native Buffalonian, but she carries the special credentials that go with having been raised in New Haven, a city that claims to have been the scene of the invention of two other American specialties — the hamburger and the American pizza. Although Leonard Katz normally limits his chicken-wing consumption to downing a few as hors d'oeuvres — a policy, he assured me, that has no connection at all with the fact that his medical specialty is the gastrointestinal tract — the rest of the family think nothing of making an entire meal out of them. Not long before I arrived in Buffalo for my field work, Linda Katz had returned from her freshman year at Washington University, in St. Louis — a city where, for reasons I do not intend to pursue, the local specialty is toasted ravioli — and headed straight for her favorite chicken-wing outlet to repair a four-month deprivation. A friend of Linda's who returned from the University of Michigan at about the same time had eaten chicken wings for dinner four nights in a row before she felt fit to carry on. Judy Katz told me that she herself eats chicken wings not only for dinner but, every now and then, for breakfast — a pattern of behavior that I think qualifies her as being somewhere between a contemporary observer and a fanatic.

On my first evening in Buffalo, the Katz family and some other contemporary observers of their acquaintance took me on a tour of what they considered a few appropriate chicken-wing sources — out of what is said to be several hundred places in the area where Buffalonians can order what they usually refer to simply as "wings" — so that I could make some preliminary research notes for later analysis. The tour naturally included the Anchor Bar, where celebrated visitors to Buffalo — say, a daughter of the Vice-President — are now taken as a matter of course, the way they are driven out to see Niagara Falls. It also included a noted chicken-wing center called Duffs and a couple of places that serve beef-on-weck — a beef sandwich on a salty roll — which happens to be the local specialty that was replaced in the hearts of true Buffalonians by chicken wings. In Buffalo, chicken wings are always offered "mild" or "medium" or "hot," depending on how much of a dose of hot sauce they have been subjected to during preparation, and they are always accompanied by celery and blue-cheese dressing. I sampled mild. I sampled medium. I sampled hot. It turned out that there is no sort of chicken wing I don't like. As is traditional, I washed down the wings with a number of bottles of Genesee or Molson — particularly when I was sampling the hot. I ate celery between chicken wings. I dipped the celery into the blue-cheese dressing.

I dipped chicken wings into the blue-cheese dressing. (I learned later that nobody in Buffalo has figured out for sure what to do with the blue-cheese dressing.) I tried a beef-on-weck, just for old times sake. I found that I needed another order of hot, plus another bottle of Molson. After four hours, the tour finally ended with Judy Katz apologizing for the fact that we were too late for her favorite chicken-wing place, a pizza parlor called Santora's, which closes at 1:00 A.M.

The next morning, I got out my preliminary research notes for analysis. They amounted to three sentences I was unable to make out, plus what appeared to be a chicken-wing stain. I showed the stain to Judy Katz. "Medium?" I asked.

"Medium or hot," she said.

Fortunately, the actual moment that Buffalo chicken wings were invented has been described many times by Frank Bellissimo and his son, Dom, with the sort of rich detail that any historian would value; unfortunately, they used different details. According to the account Frank Bellissimo often gave over the years, the invention of the Buffalo chicken wing came about because of a mistake — the delivery of some chicken wings instead of the backs and necks that were ordinarily used in making spaghetti sauce. Frank Bellissimo thought it was a shame to use the wings for sauce. "They were looking at you, like saying, 'I don't belong in the sauce,'" he often recalled. He implored his wife, who was doing the cooking, to figure out some more dignified end for the wings. Teressa Bellissimo, presumably moved by her husband's plea, decided to make the wings into some hors d'oeuvres for the bar — and the Buffalo chicken wing was born.

Dom Bellissimo is a short, effusive man who now acts as the bustling host of the Anchor Bar; his friends sometimes call him Rooster. He told me a story that did not include a mistaken delivery or, for that matter, Frank Bellissimo. According to Dom, it was late on a Friday night in 1964, a time when Roman Catholics still confined themselves to fish and vegetables on Friday. He was tending the bar. Some regulars had been spending a lot of money, and Dom asked his mother to make something special to pass around gratis at the stroke of midnight. Teressa Bellissimo picked up some chicken wings — parts of a chicken that most people do not consider even good enough to give away to barflies — and the Buffalo chicken wing was born.

According to both accounts, Teressa Bellissimo cut off and discarded the small appendage on a chicken wing that looks as if it might have been a mistake in the first place, chopped the remainder of each wing in half, and served two straight sections that the regulars at the bar could eat with their fingers. (The two straight pieces, one of which looks like a miniature drumstick and is known locally as a drumette, became one of the major characteristics of the dish; in Buffalo, a plate of wings does not look like a plate of wings but like an order of fried chicken that has, for some reason, been reduced drastically in scale.) She deep-fried them (or maybe "bake-barbecued" them), applied some hot sauce, and served them on a plate that included some celery from the Anchor Bar's regular antipasto and some of the blue-cheese dressing normally used as the house dressing for salads. If the regulars were puzzled about what to do with the blue-cheese dressing, they were presumably too grateful to say so.

The accounts of Dom and Frank also agree that the wings were an immediate success — famous throughout Buffalo within weeks. In the clipping libraries of the Buffalo newspapers, I could find only one article that dealt with the Bellissimo family and their restaurant in that period — a long piece on Frank and Teressa in the *Courier-Express* in 1969, five years after the invention of the chicken wing. It talks a lot about the musicians who appeared at the Bellissimo's restaurant over the years and about the entertainers who used to drop in after road shows. It mentions the custom Teressa and Frank had in times gone by of offering a few songs themselves late on a Saturday night — Teressa emerging from behind the pasta pots in the kitchen to belt out "Oh Marie" or "Tell Me That You Love Me." It does not mention chicken wings.

Maybe Dom and Frank Bellissimo got fuzzy on dates after some time passed. By chance, my most trusted contemporary observers, the Katzes, were living out of the city during the crucial period; Linda Katz looked surprised to hear that there had ever been a time when

people did not eat chicken wings. The exact date of
the discovery seemed a small matter, though, compared
to the central historical fact that, whatever the circumstances, the first plate of Buffalo chicken wings
emerged from the kitchen of the Anchor Bar. It seemed
to me that if a pack of revisionist historians descended
on Buffalo, itching to get their hands on some piece of
conventional wisdom to refute, they would have no
serious quarrel with the basic story of how the Buffalo
chicken wing was invented — although the feminists
among them might point out that the City of Buffalo's
proclamation would have been more accurate if it had
named as the inventor Teressa Bellissimo. The inventor
of the airplane, after all, was not the person who told
Wilbur and Orville Wright that it might be nice to have
a machine that could fly.

ॐ

"A blue-collar dish for a blue-collar town," one of the
Buffalonians who joined the Katz family and me on
our chicken-wing tour said, reminding me that an historian is obligated to put events in the context of their
setting, even if his mouth happens to be full at the time.
Buffalo does have the reputation of being a blue-collar
town — a blue-collar town that during the winter is
permanently white with snow. Buffalonians who do
much traveling have resigned themselves to the fact
that the standard response to hearing that someone
comes from Buffalo is a Polish joke or some line like

"Has the snow melted yet?" Buffalo has always had a civic morale problem; one of the T-shirts for sale in town reads "Buffalo: City of No Illusions." Now that it is common to be served a dish called "Buffalo chicken wings" in places like Boston or Atlanta, is the problem being exacerbated by Buffalo's identification with a local specialty made from what is considered to be one of the chicken's less majestic parts? Frank Bellissimo seemed to argue against that interpretation. "Anybody can sell steak," he once said. "But if you sell odds and ends of one thing or another, then you're doing something." The celebrated visitors who troop through the Anchor Bar are, after all, almost always favorably impressed by Buffalo chicken wings. Craig Claiborne, the renowned food writer for the *New York Times*, proclaimed them "excellent" in one of his columns — although he may have undercut the compliment a bit by saying in the same paragraph that he had remained in Buffalo for only three hours.

A Buffalo stockbroker named Robert M. Budin once wrote a piece for the *Courier-Express* Sunday magazine suggesting, in a lighthearted way, that the city adopt the chicken wing as its symbol. Budin's piece begins with two Buffalonians discussing what had happened when one of them was at a party in Memphis and was asked by a local where he was from. Deciding to "take him face on," the visiting Buffalonian had said, "I'm from Buffalo." Instead of asking if the snow had melted yet, the local had said, "Where those dynamite chicken wings come from?"

"You mean positive recognition?" the friend who is

hearing the story asks. It becomes obvious to the two of them that Buffalonians should "mount a campaign to associate Buffalo with chicken wings and rid ourselves of the negatives of snow and cold and the misunderstood beef-on-weck." Budin suggested that the basketball team be called the Buffalo Wings, that the mayor begin wearing a button that says "Do Your Thing With Wings," and that a huge statue of a chicken wing (medium hot) be placed in the convention center.

When I telephoned Budin to inquire about the response to his suggestion, he said it had not been overwhelming. He told me, in fact, that he had embarked on a new campaign to improve Buffalo's reputation. Budin said that a lot of people believed that the city's image suffered from its name. I remembered that his Sunday-magazine piece had ended "Buffalo, thy name is chicken wing." Surely he was not suggesting that the name of the city be changed to Chicken Wing, New York. No. What should be changed, he told me, was not the name but its pronunciation. He had taken to pronouncing the first syllable as if it were spelled "boo" — so that Buffalo rhymes with Rue de Veau. "It has a quality to it that lifts it above the prosaic 'Buffalo,' " he said.

Maybe. But I suspect that it's only a matter of time before Budin tells some corporate executive in Memphis or Cincinnati that he is calling from Boofalo and the executive says, "Has the snoo melted yet?"

ह‌•

On my last evening in Buffalo — just before the Katzes and I drove out on Niagara Falls Boulevard to try the wings at a place called Fat Man's Got 'Em, and just before I got final instructions from Judy Katz about the cardboard bucket of wings I was planning to take back to New York from Santora's the next day, in the way that a medievalist might haul home a small thirteenth-century tapestry ("Get the big bucket. Whatever's left over will be fine the next morning") — I met a man named John Young, who told me, "I am actually the creator of the wing." Young, who is black, reminded me that black people have always eaten chicken wings. What he invented, he said, was the sauce that created Buffalo chicken wings — a special concoction he calls mambo sauce. He said that chicken wings in mambo sauce became his specialty in the middle sixties, and that he even registered the name of his restaurant, John Young's Wings 'n Things, at the county courthouse before moving to Illinois in 1970.

"If the Anchor Bar was selling chicken wings, nobody in Buffalo knew it then," Young said. "After I left here, everybody started chicken wings."

Young, who had returned to Buffalo a few months before our talk, told me that those who had copied the dish must be saying, "Oh, man! The original King of the Wings is back. He's fixin' to do a job on you." In fact, Young said, he was pleased to see so many people in Buffalo make money off his invention — a magnanimous sentiment that I had also heard expressed by the Bellissimos.

The wings Young invented were not chopped in half — a process he includes in the category of "tampering with them." They were served breaded, covered in mambo sauce. It is true, a local poultry distributor told me, that John Young as well as Frank Bellissimo started buying a lot of chicken wings in the middle sixties, but there was no reason for the distributor to have kept the sales receipts that might indicate who was first. "First with what?" I thought, as I sampled an order of medium and an order of hot at Santora's while picking up my bucket-to-go. Was the Buffalo chicken wing invented when Teressa Bellissimo thought of splitting it in half and deep-frying it and serving it with celery and blue-cheese dressing? Was it invented when John Young started using mambo sauce and thought of elevating wings into a specialty? How about the black people who have always eaten chicken wings? The way John Young talked, black people may have been eating chicken wings in thirteenth-century Spain. How is it that historians can fix the date of the Battle of Agincourt with such precision? How can they be so certain of its outcome?

Divining the
Mysteries of the East

PEOPLE WHO ARE always saying that scholar-
ship is of no use in the practical business of
everyday life apparently do not know about
James D. McCawley, professor of linguistics at the University of Chicago, who is able to read the signs on the
walls of Chinese restaurants. Unlike some of the rest of
us, McCawley can enter a Chinese restaurant secure
in the knowledge that his digestion will not be impaired
by the frustration of watching Chinese customers enjoy
some succulent marvel whose name the management
has not bothered to translate into English. Unlike
some of the rest of us, McCawley does not have to subject himself to puzzled stares from Chinese families
while hovering close to their plates in an effort to
divine by shape and smell what sort of braised fish dish
seems to be making them so happy. Unlike, say, Bill

Helfrich, a man I know who moved to Bar Harbor from New York — presumably driven from the city by the agonies of monolingual eating in Chinatown — McCawley has never been reduced to carrying in his wallet a note that says in Mandarin "Please bring me some of what that man at the next table is having." McCawley can read the specials listed on the wall. Nobody can hide any crisp-skin deep-fried squab from McCawley. McCawley does not find himself inquiring in painfully enunciated English about a mysterious listing only to be dismissed by the waiter with a curt "You no like." McCawley does not have to make do with translations on the menu like "Shredded Three Kinds." McCawley does not spend half the meal staring at his neighbor's bean curd with the particularly ugly combination of greed and envy so familiar to — well, to some of the rest of us.

I realize that those who scoff at knowledge for its own sake would argue that McCawley could have learned to read Chinese without subjecting himself to three years of graduate work at M.I.T. in subjects like phonology and lexicography and semantics and syntax. He could have simply stuffed down a short course in Chinese characters at Berlitz, the scoffers would say, like some sales representative about to embark for Peking with the goal of putting a can of Reddi-Wip in every Chinese home. There is a significant difference. The true scholar shares the fruit of his research through teaching and publication. Although students who arrive at the University of Chicago to study linguistics may expect to receive as orientation material nothing more than the customary map of the campus and a list of the departmental regulations governing the use of reserved books at the main library, what they get includes a packet of half a dozen menus from Chicago Chinese restaurants "collected and translated by James D. McCawley."

The menu translations do not even constitute McCawley's most ambitious work in the field. Among his writings — most of which have titles like "The Role of Notation in Generative Phonology" or "Morphological Indeterminacy in Underlying Syntactic Structure" or "Lexicographic Notes on English Quantifiers" — is a document called "The Eaters' Guide to Chinese Characters." A 53-page typescript accompanied by a 140-page glossary, the "Eaters' Guide" uses a system of character classification adapted from the Japanese in an attempt to free the non-Chinese-speaking eater forever from the wretched restrictions of the English menu. "One of my linguist friends suggested that it might be a service to mankind," McCawley has said of the guide. "And to him in particular." McCawley has even offered to teach a course in Chinese-menu reading as part of the university's extension program, but it has apparently been delayed by some difficulties in arriving at a suitable title. According to McCawley, officials of the extension program thought that Menu Chinese was not a course title appropriate to an institution with the august academic reputation of the University of Chicago, and were not impressed when he, attempting to take their concerns into consideration, offered as an alternative title Aristotle, Freud, and the Chinese Menu.

It seems to me that McCawley's scholarly achievements in the field of Chinese menus are all the more impressive in view of the fact that he doesn't happen to speak Chinese. His doctoral thesis required him to learn Japanese, and many Japanese characters are close to Chinese characters — or were before some postwar modifications in Chinese writing that, fortunately for McCawley, a lot of owners of American Chinese restaurants were not in China to find out about. Starting in the early seventies, McCawley simply built on his knowledge of Japanese characters, with the help of a lot of research into Chinese cookbooks and some extensive field work in Chinese restaurants — during which, for all we know, someone who did not fully understand McCawley's goals and methods might have been saying, "You're making an absolute pig of yourself."

I suppose some people might consider "The Eaters' Guide to Chinese Characters" the product of a hobby, albeit a hobby that happens to result in a service to mankind, but I'm happy to say that McCawley doesn't see it that way. He does not draw severe distinctions between his outside interests — principally food and music — and the field in which he makes his living. A lot of his colleagues seem to feel the same way — linguistics being, for one reason or another, a field that attracts a lot of musicians who like to eat. A graduate student of linguistics whom I met with McCawley —

we were all eating in a Korean restaurant — told me that when she was studying at the University of Michigan the newsletter of the Linguistics Department seemed to consist mainly of recipes. At the annual party McCawley throws for St. Cecilia's Day, honoring the patron saint of musicians, he is ordinarily able to put together a small orchestra of linguists. (The other annual party he gives is on October 9, in celebration of the only national holiday anywhere having to do with linguistics — the commemoration in Korea of the day in 1446 when han'gul, the Korean alphabet, was officially adopted.) When McCawley's students and colleagues published a sort of antic festschrift in his honor in 1971 — it was called "Studies Out in Left Field: Defamatory Essays Presented to James D. Mc-Cawley on the Occasion of his 33rd or 34th Birthday," and it included a large section called "Pornolinguistics and Scatolinguistics" — the title on the cover was superimposed on the menu of a Chinese restaurant. In the same spirit as the festschrift, McCawley once presented to the University of Chicago Hillel Foundation's annual Latke-Homantash Symposium a paper on "Some Hitherto Unrecognized Implications of the Chinese Terms for Latkes and Homentashen" — although after several readings I'm not certain I understand precisely what those implications are.

I suspect that part of what has led McCawley's students and colleagues to admire him enough to do a festschrift in his honor is his ability to discover a scholarly meeting, a concert, and an interesting restau-

rant in the same city at the same time. Discussing the
Philosophy of Science Association meeting in Toronto,
he may digress on the advantages of having a Toronto
colleague whose research in Chinese syntax has en-
abled him to know that the proprietors of what seems
to be a Szechuan restaurant on Spadina Avenue are
actually natives of Jiangxi Province who can, upon request, turn out a proper Jiangxi banquet. Right in his
own department, of course, McCawley has access to
colleagues who, for example, may have done enough
field work in the dialects of southeastern Europe to
become expert in Greek cuisine, and he has no rigid
notions of interdepartmental rivalry that might pre-
vent him from dipping into the Department of Far
Eastern Languages and Civilizations if the need should
arise. Not all members of the Linguistics Department,
after all, have a particular interest in foreign languages
or foreign cultures or even foreign food; even those who
do may have acquired expertise from their field work
that is not obviously transferable to the gastronomic
challenges of Chicago. For instance, one of McCawley's
colleagues, Jerrold Sadock, has done a lot of work on
Greenlandic Eskimo, and there are as yet no Greenlandic Eskimo restaurants in Chicago. It is not a cuisine
whose absence distresses McCawley, since the recipe
Sadock remembers best begins, "Kill and gut one seal,
stuff the body cavity with auks, sew up, bury in sand,
dig up in six months."

A scholar who makes no priggish distinction between knowledge of phonology and knowledge of latkes is obviously my sort of scholar. From the first time I heard about McCawley, I figured I could learn a lot from him. Although the course he teaches in the Linguistics Department at the University of Chicago, Justification of Linguistic Units, sounds worthwhile, the course I was hoping to get a head start on was Aristotle, Freud, and the Chinese Menu. I have been frustrated for years by the Chinese wall signs in Chinatown. I have publicly admitted that when Alice taught a class at City College which included some Chinese students not long in this country I suggested wall-sign translation as an exercise that might be just the thing for polishing their idiomatic English. I have also revealed in public print that I often have fantasies of having been selected by the State Department to take Mao Tse-tung on eating tours of New York that include Chinatown — and that Mao always brings along his interpreter. On trips to Chinatown with my family, I was becoming increasingly sensitive about the fact that whenever I leaped from my chair to follow some waiter who passed by carrying an obviously fantastic bean-curd dish resembling nothing described on the English menu my daughters tended to say "Daddy — please" in the same way Sarah says "Daddy — please" to indicate that she finds it embarrassing to walk to the grocery store with someone who happens to be singing "The Streets of Laredo." I needed help.

The first time I caught up with McCawley was when

he was on a visit to New York. As I understood the purpose of the visit, he had agreed to deliver a lecture called "The Nonexistence of Syntactic Categories" at Columbia University and at the Bell Laboratories, he was desperately interested in attending two Janácek operas that the City Opera was going to produce on successive evenings, and he wanted to sample the goat curry at a Trinidadian restaurant on Nostrand Avenue in Brooklyn. I had arranged to fly back to Chicago with him, for a sort of short-course in his methodology, and I suggested that we meet the day before our flight for a tea lunch at a place in Chinatown called H.S.F. — giving him a chance to pick up some Chinese ingredients at the Kam Man supermarket on Canal Street and giving me a chance to get some translation done closer to home than Chicago.

My translation needs at H.S.F. did not have to do with menus. Tea-lunch — or dim-sum — restaurants are about the only places in Chinatown that do not drive me mad with linguistic frustration, since the food-service system common to all of them might almost have been designed to soothe the fears of monolingual gluttons. Waiters pass up and down the aisles with carts or trays holding small plates of dumplings or shrimp balls or noodles or some other dim-sum specialty, the customer takes a plate of whatever appeals to him, and a waiter slightly senior to the passers arrives at the table at the end of the meal to tally up the bill by counting the number of plates on the table — a system that somehow does not tempt too many customers to gain the double benefit of more china and a smaller bill by slipping some of the plates into their pockets. Although I have never met a dim-sum passer who spoke English well enough to explain what was inside the dumplings he was passing, my method of eating a tea lunch requires no Chinese: I simply take some of absolutely everything offered.

My purpose in luring McCawley to H.S.F. was based on a suspicion that a Chinese wall sign I had noticed there was in fact not a list of special dishes but an explanation of some changes in the restaurant which had struck some of its customers as distinctly un-Chinatown. H.S.F. used to be called Hee Seung Fung. Not long after it started going by its initials, it was redecorated in a rather sleek style that was conspicuously lacking in both dragons and pagodas. It opened a branch uptown. For a time, it made some of its dim sum available in frozen form at Bloomingdale's. I figured that the wall sign said something reassuring to Chinese-speaking customers — "Don't be put off by the trendy flash done for the benefit of the wide eyes, because we're still just folks," or words to that effect.

McCawley turned out to be a man with a heavy mustache, full sideburns, and shoulder-length dark hair. He looked like a sixties radical gone not quite respectable. He had lived in Glasgow until he was six and in Chicago after that — giving him a way of speaking so much his own that it is probably of no interest to those of his sociolinguistic colleagues who study accents and dialects. I explained the task at hand as we entered H.S.F.

"Two?" the waiter who approached us said.

McCawley stopped in his tracks and stared at the wall sign. "The first column says black-bean steam fish something or other," he said. "Whatever that last character is."

"Are you sure it doesn't say anything about Bloomingdale's?" I asked.

McCawley, without saying whether or not he knew the Chinese character for Bloomingdale's, assured me that the wall sign simply listed some of the specialties that could be ordered at dinner. He tried the first column again. Turning to the waiter who had greeted us, he said, "What the bloody hell is that last character?"

The waiter looked blank for a moment. Then he said again, "Two?"

ॐ

Until I spent a couple of days in the company of James McCawley, I had not thought of Chicago as an Oriental city. Among wandering eaters, it is probably best known for the pirouettes its restaurants manage in what other cities think of as the straightforward business of turning out pizzas. It seems to me that over the years a lot of the conversations I have had in Chicago have concerned authentic Chicago pizza or deep-dish pizza or double-crusted pizza or a pizzalike object known as a panzerotti. The fame of Chicago pizza now extends well beyond the city limits. There are places in London jammed with Englishmen eating Chicago pizza in an atmosphere distinguished by Cubs pennants and framed front pages of the *Chicago Daily News* and election posters urging yet another term for Richard Daley. The sort of pizza our friend Fats Goldberg, the thin New York pizza baron, began serving in Manhattan in the sixties was the Chicago version of the beast. It was in Chicago that the Fat Man, then beginning his business career as a 320–pound advertising space salesman for the *Tribune*, summoned up a will power that nobody who had ever witnessed him stop for a Kresge chili-dog on the way to lunch could have believed he possessed, and lost weight at a rate that eventually turned him into half of the Fats Goldberg I once knew. Fats claims that he developed his own recipe for Chicago pizza, but he acknowledges that, like most disciples who have carried the Chicago version to the outside world, he took a crack or two at stealing the recipe developed by a pioneering Chicago parlor called Pizzeria Uno. According to Fats, the plan was for him to stand in the alley next to Uno's kitchen, pretending to spoon with a volunteer sweetie while glancing regularly through the window to absorb the secrets of the craft. What the Fat Man had neglected to consider in planning his operation was the cold wind coming off Lake Michigan in February; the volunteer didn't mind a little necking, but she had not signed up for frostbite. The ersatz lovebirds abandoned their post before the pepperoni went on.

McCawley doesn't talk much about pizza or any other foodstuff with origins in Europe. He alone seems to treat Chicago as a sort of prairie Hong Kong. His "Notes on Access to Interesting Food in Chicago," prepared for the students and faculty of the Linguistics Department, lists as its ethnic categories Chinese, Japanese, Korean, Thai, Indian, and Other. He was able to pick his way through an Indian menu pretty well even before he started studying Hindi in preparation for a trip to India he was planning to take a few months after my visit. Although he celebrates Korean han'gul more confidently than he reads it, a steady supply of han'gul readers seems assured by the fact that Koreans are particularly drawn to graduate studies in linguistics — a natural result, perhaps, of being let out of school year after year in honor of an alphabet. In addition to a fair-sized Chinatown, Chicago has any number of Korean restaurants and several Thai restaurants and a clutch of Indian restaurants, including one valued so highly by the linguistics crowd that it has catered the annual meeting of the Chicago Linguistics Society. With McCawley in Chicago, I ate Mutter Panir at the Moti Mahal Restaurant, and Yook Hoi at a Korean restaurant called Cho Sun Ok, and Panang Nue at Friend, a Thai restaurant — all the while confident that I was eating what I was intended to eat rather than some chop-suey equivalent put on the English menu to pacify the passing meter reader or paper-supply salesman who happened to drop by because he suddenly got hungry while on his rounds. McCawley would simply find a scrap of paper (usually a deposit slip from his checkbook), write our order in the appropriate alphabet, and hand it to the waiter along with an English "Thank you."

Our Chinese meal was at a place called Chinese Deli. Its non-English-speaking customers presumably call it something else. When we discussed names given to Chinese restaurants — I admitted to a weakness for the name of a Los Angeles place called Yangzee Doodle — McCawley said that in Australia he once came upon a restaurant that was called Epping Chinese Restaurant in English and was identified by its Chinese characters as a restaurant called Occidental Food. A wall sign in the Chinese Deli listed all sorts of dishes that were not on the English menu. Among the delicacies available to readers of Chinese characters, McCawley announced, were chicken feet with black beans, and salted mustard greens with goose intestines. I like to think that I'm as fond of chicken feet as the next fellow, but goose intestines are the sort of thing that makes me suspect that those Chinese waiters were correct a number of times when they said, "You no like." I put aside my doubts. The store of mankind's knowledge was not expanded by scholars who failed to seek because of fear of what they might find. "These goose intestines are not bad," I said to McCawley when our meal had been delivered. The sincerity of the compliment was not really undercut, it seems to me, by the possibility that I was eating the Chicago version of chicken feet.

McCawley had been kind enough to give me a copy of "The Eaters' Guide to Chinese Characters," and I intended to apply myself to learning how to use it. "Will I really be able to read the wall signs in Chinatown?" I asked.

"If they're printed," McCawley said. "Script is a little more difficult." The growing use of modern Chinese modifications adds another difficulty, he explained, not to speak of the euphemisms that Chinese often use in describing food. For instance, before we left H.S.F., McCawley had told me that the final character in the sign he found troublesome was "cloud," which might have been a euphemism for fish stomach or might not have been. Later, he decided it was a nonstandard character for wonton.

On the way back to New York, I studied the guide. It looked as if it required about the application necessary to get through a graduate course in phonology at M.I.T. Also, if even McCawley sometimes had difficulty telling characters apart, it was obvious that a novice might often order what appeared to be wonton only to be brought fish stomach — fish stomach he would have to eat unless he wanted to risk having the waiter come over to say, "I told you you no like." Linguistic research began to seem even more complicated than history. I decided I would ask McCawley to do one more translation for me, from English to Chinese — a note that said, "Please bring me some of what that man at the next table is having."

Confessions of a
Stand-Up Sausage Eater

I SUPPOSE I would have given up the Feast of
San Gennaro years ago if I'd had any choice. San
Gennaro has always been the largest Italian
festival in the city, and for a long time now Mulberry
Street during the Feast has been crowded enough to
give the impression that, for reasons lost to history,
Manhattan folk customs include an annual outdoor
enactment of precisely the conditions present in the
I.R.T. uptown express during rush hour. In September,
the weather in New York can be authentically Neapolitan — particularly on a street that is jammed with
people and sealed on both sides with a line of stands
where venders are boiling oil for zeppole or barbecuing
braciole over charcoal. Occasionally, I have become
irritated with the Feast even on evenings when I have
no intention of attending it, since I have become one

of those Manhattan residents who get testy when some event brings even more traffic than usual into the city from the suburbs. Those of us who migrated to New York from the middle of the country may be even less tolerant of incursions by out-of-towners than the natives are, and I suppose I might as well admit that, in some particularly frustrating gridlock on some particularly steamy fall day, I may have shouted, "Go back where you came from, you rubes!" in the direction of a lot of former New Yorkers who now live a mile or two into New Jersey — an outburst that would have been even ruder if the objects of my irritation had not been safely encased in soundproof air-conditioned cars. The traffic congestion caused by San Gennaro is particularly irritating to me because Mulberry Street lies between our house and Chinatown, and the Feast happens to fall at the time of year when I return to the city from a summer in Nova Scotia suffering the anguish of extended Chinese-food deprivation. For Occidentals, we eat very well in Nova Scotia. Around the middle of August, though, even as I'm plowing through a feast that may include mushroom soup made from wild mushrooms we have gathered in the woods and halibut just off the boat and sugar-snap peas so sweet that even Sarah (whose last recorded expression of enthusiasm for eating anything green came at a street fair that was selling green cotton candy) has been witnessed eating them straight off the vine and freshly baked bread and blueberry pie made from wild blueberries, I become acutely aware of how many miles, nautical and overland, stand between me and Mott Street.

Practically feverish with visions of crabs sloshing around in black-bean sauce, I detour around the Feast in a journey that seems to get longer every year, as the lights of San Gennaro push farther and farther uptown from the heart of Little Italy toward Houston Street, on the edge of the Lower East Side. It would not surprise me, I think, if one of these years commuters from Westchester County pouring out of Grand Central Station some hot September morning walked smack into a line of calzone and sausage stands that had crept up in an unbroken line fifty blocks from Grand Street. The venders, dishing out food as fast as they can, will still have time to complain to the account executives and bank managers they're serving about having been assigned a spot too far from the busiest blocks of the Feast.

I love the elements of San Gennaro that still exist from its origin as a neighborhood festival transplanted practically intact from Naples by Little Italy immigrants — the statue of the saint with dollar bills pinned beneath it, for instance, and the brass band that seems to consist of a half-dozen aging Italians and one young Chinese trumpet player — but the Feast has felt considerably less like a neighborhood celebration in recent years, partly because its size has inevitably brought along some atmosphere of mass production, partly because of the inclusion of such non-Neapolitan specialties as piña coladas and eggrolls and computer portraits, and partly because of the self-consciousness represented by "Kiss Me — I'm Italian" buttons. Also, I find that I can usually catch the brass band during the year around the Chinatown part of Mulberry, below Canal Street; it often works Chinese funerals. The gambling at the Feast does not attract me, and the stuffed animals that are awarded for making a basket or knocking down milk bottles hold no appeal for someone whose family policy on stuffed animals is moving slowly, in the face of some resistance, toward what the Metropolitan Museum of Art used to call deaccessioning.

Still, there I am at San Gennaro every year — admitting to myself that I rather enjoy pushing my way down Mulberry at a time when Neapolitan music is coming over the loudspeakers and operators of games of chance are making their pitches and food smells from a dozen different booths are competing in the middle of the street. My presence is easily explained: I can't stay away from the sausage sandwiches.

As it happens, we live right around the corner from the South Village, an Italian neighborhood where the sort of sausage sandwiches served at Italian feasts — hot or sweet sausage jammed into a roll with a combination of fried pepper and onions as dressing — can be bought any day of the year in comfortable surroundings, which may even include a stool at the counter. I never buy one. Somehow, it has been clear to me since I came to the city that uncontrolled, year-round eating of sausage sandwiches is not an acceptable

option for me. It was instinct more than conscious decision — the sort of instinct that some animals must
use to know how many of certain berries to eat in the
woods. Alice, who at our house acts as enforcer for the
nutrition mob, has never had to speak on the subject
of how much devastation a steady diet of Italian sausage
could wreak on the human body. The limits are set. I
have a sausage sandwich whenever I go to San Gennaro. I have a sausage sandwich at the Feast of St.
Anthony, on Sullivan Street, in the spring. If I'm lucky,
I might stumble across one of the smaller Italian feasts
in Little Italy — I always come back from Chinatown
by a circuitous route through there, just on the off-
chance — or find a sausage stand that has attached
itself to some Village block party. Otherwise, I do
without. When I go back for visits to Kansas City, my
hometown, and I'm asked by my old high-school friends
how I possibly survive in New York, I tell them that
the way I survive is simple: I only eat sausage sandwiches standing up.

I am not the only seasonal eater in New York. There
is a time in the fall when a lot of people who have spent
August in some rural setting — talking a lot of brave
talk about how there is nothing better than a simple
piece of broiled fish and some absolutely fresh vegetables — come back to the city and head straight for
the sort of food that seems to exist only in close
proximity to cement. One September, I noticed one of
them while I was waiting in line at Joe's Dairy on
Sullivan Street — right across the street from St.

Anthony's, the church that sponsors my spring sausage eating. As it happened, my own mission was seasonal — although one sort of business or another takes me to Joe's all year round. In the early fall, when farmers are still bringing their produce into Manhattan for Saturday-morning markets, it is possible to make a stop at the farmer's market in the West Village, pick up some basil and some tomatoes that actually taste like tomatoes rather than Christmas decorations, stop in at Joe's for mozzarella so fresh that it is still oozing milk, and put the tomatoes and mozzarella and basil and some olive oil together to create something that tastes almost too good to be described as salad. The man in front of me at Joe's Dairy was looking around the shelves as if he were a Russian defector getting his first look at Bloomingdale's. He asked for Parmesan cheese. He asked for Romano. He bought some mozzarella. "Jesus Christ! I just had a roast-pork sandwich at Frank's!" he suddenly said. "Boy, am I glad to be back in the city!" Everybody in the store nodded in sympathy.

ह≫

When I walk down Mulberry Street, just below Canal, during the Feast of San Gennaro, I am strongly affected by what I suppose could be called border tensions: I feel the competing pulls of sausage sandwiches and flounder Fukienese style. The street just east of Mulberry is Mott, the main drag of Chinatown. There was a time not many years ago when Mott and a few side streets seemed to constitute a small Chinese outpost in the middle of a large Italian neighborhood; those were the days when a Chinese candidate for the New York State Assembly endeared himself to me by telling a reporter from the *Times* that he was running against the Italian incumbent — Louis DeSalvio, the permanent grand marshal of the Feast of San Gennaro — even though he realized that he didn't have "a Chinaman's chance." Over the past ten or fifteen years, though, a surge of Chinese immigration has revitalized Chinatown and pushed out its boundaries — past the Bowery and then East Broadway in one direction, across Mulberry Street in the other. On Mulberry Street below Canal, the calzone stands and beer carts of San Gennaro stand in front of Chinese butcher shops and Chinese importing companies and Chinese produce stores. "They left us three blocks," an official of San Gennaro told me while discussing the Chinese expansion. The blocks between Canal and Broome are still dominated by the robust Italian restaurants that represent the tomato-sauce side against the forces of Northern Italian cream sauce in what has been called the War of the Red and the White. Even on those blocks of Mulberry, though, some of the windows of second-floor offices have sprouted Chinese writing. There are a lot of Italians left in the tenements of Mulberry Street, but a lot of Italians have moved away — returning only temporarily to shop on Grand Street or sit in one of the coffeehouses or eat sausage sandwiches at the Feast of San Gennaro. The Feast is still run by the grandson of the man who founded the Society of San Gennaro, Napoli e Dintorni, in 1926, but he lives on Staten Island.

Foreign food — non-Italian food, that is — began to creep into San Gennaro and some of the other Italian feasts several years ago, but not from Chinatown. There were some Korean booths and an occasional taco stand and some stands at which Filipinos sold barbecued meat on a stick and fried rice and lo mein and egg rolls and an unusual fritter that was made with vegetables and fried in oil. When I first came across the foreign booths, I decided that the purist belief in restricting Italian festivals to Italian food was narrow-minded and artificial — a decision that was based, I admit, on a certain fondness for the vegetable fritters. These days, any street event in New York — a merchants' fair on Third Avenue, a block party on the West Side — is certain to have at least one Filipino food stand, and a feast the size of San Gennaro will have half a dozen. At the annual One World Festival sponsored by the Armenian diocese — a festival that has always been so aggressively ecumenical that I wouldn't be surprised to discover someday that a few spots had been assigned to food stands run by Turks — the stands selling Armenian lahmajun and boereg and yalanchi and lule kebab seem almost outnumbered by stands selling what are sometimes called "Filipino and Polynesian specialties." The man in charge of assigning spots for San Gennaro once told me that if no attempt were made to maintain a balance — and a Feast that is not overwhelmingly Italian would obviously be unbalanced — Mulberry Street would have ten Filipino stands on every block. I have asked Filipino venders how they accounted for so many of their countrymen being in the street-fair game, but their explanations have never gone much beyond the theory that some people made money at some street fairs in brownstone neighborhoods and other people decided to get in on a good thing. It may remain one of those New York ethnic mysteries that outlanders were not meant to understand. Why are so many fruit-and-vegetable stores that were once run by Italians and so many fruit-and-vegetable stores that previously didn't exist run by Koreans? Why have I never seen a black sanitation man? Why are conversations among venders of hot dogs at the Central Park Zoo conducted in Greek?

ह∾

Selecting my sausage sandwich at San Gennaro requires a certain amount of concentration. At San Gennaro, after all, there are always at least thirty stands selling sausage sandwiches. I don't mean that I do nothing else at the Feast. In the spirit of fostering intergroup harmony, I sometimes have a vegetable fritter. I often have a few zeppole — holeless doughnuts that are available almost exclusively at Italian feasts. I have a couple of beers, muttering about the price, or some wine with fruit. Mainly, though, I inspect sausage stands — walking slowly the length of the Feast and maybe back again before I make my choice. About halfway through my inspection, I can expect to be told by another member of the party — Abigail and Sarah are ordinarily the other members of the party — that all sausage stands look alike, or maybe even that all sausage sandwiches taste alike. I tell them that they certainly weren't raised to believe that all sausage sandwiches taste alike. I tell them that their expertise in this matter is seriously limited by the refusal of either of them to taste an Italian-sausage sandwich. I remind them that a researcher who is satisfied with a less than adequate sampling risks flawed results. I keep looking.

The stands always look familiar to me. A lot of the food venders at Italian feasts in Manhattan make a business of going from feast to feast around the New York area from spring to fall. In Little Italy, it is assumed that the food-stand operators spend the rest of the year in Florida, living like kings off the sort of profits that must be accumulated by anyone who sells a tiny plate of ziti with tomato sauce for three dollars cash and doesn't have to furnish so much as a chair or a counter top. Among New Yorkers, it is practically an article of faith that anyone who runs what seems to be a small seasonal business — the ice-cream man in the park, for instance — can be found on any cold day in February casually blowing hundreds of dollars at some Florida dog track. Although I recognize the stands, I can never seem to keep in my mind which one has served me the best sausage sandwich. The last time I went to San Gennaro, the final inspection was carried out on a rainy weekday evening in the company of both Abigail and Sarah. I was convinced that the stand I had patronized at St. Anthony's the previous spring — acquiring a sandwich the memory of which I carried with me through the summer — was called by someone's first name. All the sausage stands at San Gennaro seemed to be called by someone's first name. Had it been Dominic's? The Original Jack's? Rocky & Philly's? Tony's? Angelo's? Smokin' Joe's? Staten Island Frank's? Gizzo's? Lucy's?

There was nothing to do but inspect each stand — Abigail and Sarah tagging along behind me, already full of pasta. I looked for a stand that was frying the sausages on a griddle rather than grilling them over charcoal — and displaying peppers and onions that had been sliced and cooked precisely to my requirements. It was amazing how many sausage stands qualified. My daughters began to remind me that it was a school night. I told them that I would write them notes if they overslept the next morning ("Abigail had to be up late to take advantage of an unusual opportunity to observe the process of pure research"). Under some pressure, I stopped in front of Staten Island Frank's — or maybe it was the Original Jack's; even now the names run together — and said, "This is it." When I started to eat, I was convinced that I had chosen brilliantly — until we passed a stand that I hadn't noticed before. It was serving sausages, with correctly fried peppers and onions, on marvelous-looking rolls that had sesame seeds on top of them.

"Sesame-seed rolls!" I said. "Nobody told me about sesame-seed rolls!"

"Take it easy," Abigail said, giving me a reassuring pat on the arm. "You can have one on a sesame-seed roll next year."

"Not next year," I reminded her as we headed home. "At St. Anthony's in June."

An Attempt to
Compile the Definitive History
of Didee's Restaurant

MY FIELD WORK IN BUFFALO was not actually my first fling at historical research. I once went to Louisiana determined to write the definitive history of Didee's restaurant, or to eat an awful lot of baked duck and dirty rice trying. I'm quick to take up scholarly challenges in southern Louisiana. Once, I went to Mamou, Louisiana, to observe the Cajun Mardi Gras celebration because I had heard that the traditional ride of Cajun horsemen around the countryside in search of chickens for the Mardi Gras chicken gumbo often comes to a halt so that the celebrants can drink beer and eat boudin. The Cajun Mardi Gras happens to be a particularly jovial event, but I have to say that I would observe the annual conference of the society of water-treatment-plant engineers if I had reason to believe that it was interrupted every so often so that the participants could drink beer and eat boudin. At the Mamou Mardi Gras, I ate a lot of boudin while I was standing in fields chosen as rest stops — squeezing the mixture of pork and seasoning and rice out of the sausage casing with one hand and holding the washdown can of beer in the other. It wasn't far from my normal style of boudin eating; I normally down boudin while standing in the parking lot of some Cajun grocery store that has managed to snatch me off the road by displaying in its window a hand-lettered sign that says "Hot Boudin Today." The Mamou boudin seemed particularly good, although I may have simply been in a particularly good mood because of the knowledge that even after all the boudin was gone we still had the chicken gumbo to look forward to. As I ate boudin in Mamou, it occurred to me that if sausage fanciers ever have our own annual conference I might find myself responding to a panel of experts who had concluded that there is little in common between boudin and East Coast Italian sausage by rising to remind the panel that both are normally eaten standing up.

Trying to compile the definitive history of Didee's restaurant wasn't easy. In fact, I might have given up the history game right there if it hadn't been for the baked duck and dirty rice. The event that had attracted my attention obviously qualified as what historians are always calling the End of an Era — the perfect moment to slip in with a definitive history. The proprietor of a tiny, family-run restaurant in a nearly abandoned section of Baton Rouge's black commercial district — Didee's, a name that had represented stupefying baked duck in Louisiana for this entire century — had sold name, duck recipe, and franchise rights to a go-go New York miniconglomerate that talked about making him "the Colonel Sanders of the duck business." All of that may strike professional historians as a simple enough tale of American commerce, but once I had arrived at Didee's and begun my research — interviewing the proprietor, Herman Perrodin, while downing a bowl of his seafood gumbo and feeling grateful for my working conditions — I realized that no tale involving Herman Perrodin was likely to be a simple tale. There was no doubt that his grandfather, Charles Adrian Lastrapes, founded the original Didee's in Opelousas, Louisiana, around the turn of the century — Perrodin's mother, Clara Lastrapes Perrodin, and her husband opened a separate Didee's in Baton Rouge in 1952 — but Herman Perrodin did not fit snugly into the role of an unspoiled folk chef nurturing an old family recipe. A tall man in his fifties with a sort of lubricated manner of talking, Perrodin occasionally described himself as a "poor little old dumb boy born in a sweet-potato patch in Opelousas, Louisiana," but he also described himself as being a better chef than Paul Bocuse. "La nouvelle cuisine!" he said to me, drawing out the last word in astonishment at the sort of thing dumb folks will believe. "Don't tell *me* about la nouvelle cuisine! I've been doing la nouvelle cuisine all my goddamn life!"

The early history of Didee's restaurant, Perrodin assured me, was not all that complicated. Charles Adrian Lastrapes started serving baked duck and baked chicken and Creole gumbo and oyster loaves while running what newspaper features about Didee's usually refer to as a coffee shop and what Perrodin figured for a gambling den or a bootlegging operation. Lastrapes was always known as Didee, pronounced to rhyme with high tea — a meal, I hardly need add, that anyone fortunate enough to eat the daily fare of Opelousas would undoubtedly regard as some form of corporal punishment. Opelousas is about sixty miles west of Baton Rouge, in the section of Louisiana long dominated by the French — an area where a noted gumbo is discussed with the seriousness it deserves, and where a lot of black and white people seem to have the same last names as well as approximately the same complexions, and where attitudes toward the more enjoyable of the Seven Deadly Sins are the sort of stuff sermons are made of in Shreveport. Didee's was always a restaurant for white people, although the Lastrapes were what are sometimes called "people of color," or Creoles. There are those in Louisiana who object to the word "Creole" being used to designate people of mixed race rather than the white descendants of the Colonial French, and there are those in Louisiana who believe that people who serve the sort of baked duck that Didee Lastrapes and his second wife, Miz Anna, put out for so many years in a little restaurant just off the courthouse square in Opelousas can call themselves anything they please.

"This is edible gumbo," I said, while Perrodin paused between stories of a childhood in Didee's kitchen and stories of his wanderings around the country after he left Opelousas as a teenager ("I'm the traveling, adventurous, aggressive black sheep of the family"). He agreed that the gumbo was at least superb. In southern Louisiana, it is customary for a serious cook to assume the preeminence of his version of anything. Perrodin's son, Charles, who struck me as relatively reserved, said to me later that day, "You ever taste our shrimp étouffée? You taste our étouffée, you'll throw rocks at other people's étouffée."

Didee Lastrapes died in the mid-forties, Perrodin said, but the Opelousas restaurant remained open under Miz Anna's stewardship until her death in 1970.

"Then Dee Dee's opened where Didee's had been," I said, introducing a complication I already knew about and opening what I believe the methodology specialists at the American Historical Association conferences refer to among themselves as a real bucket of worms.

Perrodin dismissed Dee Dee's with a wave of his hand.

What happened, I knew, was that Thomas and Tony Blouin, who had worked for Miz Anna for years, reopened the restaurant, choosing the name Dee Dee's for reasons Thomas Blouin once summarized pithily for a visiting reporter: "So people would know it's the same but different." I once ate at Dee Dee's. In 1972, Alice and I stopped in Opelousas on our way — well, more or less on our way — to the Breaux Bridge crawfish festival. I remember Alice speculating on the ingredients in the dirty rice, in the tone of voice a bomb-squad man might use to discuss how the terrorists rigged up something small enough to fit into a satchel but powerful enough to destroy a wing of the post office. As I remember, we had a fine meal, although I may have simply been in a particularly good mood because of the knowledge that even after the duck was gone we had the crawfish to look forward to.

"Did you think the food was any good at Dee Dee's?" I asked Perrodin.

He waved his hand again. "A lot of people can do things and a lot of people have to be directed," he said. "It went kerplop, and now they're cooking on the off-shore oil rigs or something."

For most of the history we had been discussing, Perrodin was not what the historians call a primary source. The wanderings he had begun as a teenager kept him out of Louisiana until he went to Baton Rouge for a few years in the late fifties to help out his father, Arlington Perrodin, as a sort of catering manager. Perrodin told me that the jobs he had held around the country as a waiter or bartender or cook or manager would take four years to list. He could present a ten-minute declamation on what he learned along the way about which tastes are received where in what he called "the sculpture of the mouth" or on what he learned about herbs alone ("I'm like a perfumer. I mean it. I'm telling you. I studied the herbs for five years. I could tell you more about herbs than the man who wrote the book"). He could also present a declamation on the high life, and on the personal lesson he learned when he was sent to prison in Texas in 1970 as a heroin user. Perrodin talked about his drug habit the way he talked about his gumbo. One minute, while mentioning the last spice in a recipe that gives it "that zing — *respect,* I call it," he would slam his hand on the table and say, *"Voilà!* Now I got your whole mouth lit up!" A few minutes later, he would fling both hands toward the ceiling and say, "A quarter of a million dollars flowed through these arms!"

When Arlington Perrodin died in 1976, a few years after Herman had come home for good, Didee's was not far from kerplop itself. It had been mentioned in national magazines; movie stars had written raves in its guestbook; the Confrérie de la Chaîne des Rôtisseurs (le Chapitre de Nouvelle-Orleans) had included on one of its formal menus "Canard à la Didee, Rize au Fave, Les 'Mustard Greens.'" But not many Baton Rouge people came to eat. The neighborhood was evaporating around Didee's, and Herman Perrodin could not seem to raise the capital to move or even to advertise. "You can't do anything without money," Perrodin said. "Cash money. No checks."

In 1974, a review by Richard Collin in the *New Orleans States-Item* suggesting that Didee's would flourish if it moved to New Orleans had resulted in a number of proposals, but every one of them had fallen through. During the last year of Arlington Perrodin's life, Herman took a fling at a scheme by some young Baton Rouge entrepreneurs to feature Didee's cooking in Aspen — a flop from which he acquired nothing but an interest in skiing to add to his taste for the high life. There were other offers, but Perrodin dismissed them as schemes in which he might do a lot of work without seeing any money. "I'm not waitin' for no net," he explained to me. "You can have all the net you want. Give me the gross."

After three-quarters of a century of his family's building the reputation of Didee's, the way Perrodin analyzed it, he had found himself in the position of an unappreciated and — even worse — undercompensated genius. There was Paul Bocuse, according to Perrodin's calculations, making fifteen thousand dollars for catering a meal, and there was Herman Perrodin doing all of his own cooking and ordering and bill paying and, sometimes, sweeping up — and still never taking in more than a few hundred dollars on a good day. "I got obligations and I got a life-style," Perrodin told me. "I'm not satisfied with the way I'm living. I'm not satisfied with the home I live in. I'm not satisfied with the car I drive."

Enter Omni Capital Worldwide, Ltd., go-go mini-conglomerate whose name might be taken as another way of saying, "All Money Everywhere."

I had lunch at Didee's with Herb Turner, who had moved to Baton Rouge from Fort Lauderdale a couple of years before to run Omni Capital's operations in Louisiana. Turner struck me as very go-go himself. He said he had been so busy that he hadn't had time to get rid of his second Cadillac before buying his third. The previous few days had been particularly hectic, he said, because he had a guest in town — a very close personal friend who happened to be Frank Sinatra's bodyguard.

I knew I was digressing from the history of Didee's, but I couldn't resist the obvious question: "Who's watching Frank?"

"Frank's OK," Turner said, digressing himself into show business for some encouraging stories about Eddie Fisher's comeback. As it happens, Fisher once ate at Didee's, and left a rude remark about Elizabeth Taylor in the guestbook. Arlington Perrodin covered that page with clear plastic for protection.

Omni Capital, Turner told me, had been founded in New York as a tax-shelter consulting business by one investment banker who was also a CPA, and another who was also a Hollywood booking agent. In describing its history, he and another Omni executive who had joined us for lunch used the word "roll" a lot. They talked about rolling out of tax shelters into film distribution, and rolling out of timberland into housing developments. It seemed natural enough to roll out of housing developments into baked duck and dirty rice. In fact, on those rare evenings when I find myself in a place where the only alternative to sitting like a condemned man in the motel dining room is starvation, rolling into baked duck and dirty rice is something I've thought about a lot myself.

What Omni was planning, Turner said, was to build a prototype Didee's near the Baton Rouge Country Club — a Garden Room that could be adapted for private parties, an Acadian Room with beams of distressed wood, a good bar. If the prototype succeeded, Didee's Famous Restaurant, Inc., the corporation formed for the occasion, would start franchising. Turner said Omni planned to send out Didee credit cards, carrying preferential reservation privileges, to five thousand business contacts in the state. "That'll take care of that," he said. "I can't imagine the general public getting a shot at that restaurant."

"The duck is delicious," I said to Perrodin. I happen to like duck. I don't think I like it as well as Alice does. When it comes to partiality to ducks, Alice is outdone by nobody except, perhaps, other ducks. In the jockeying that goes on during the decision-making concerning what dishes are to be ordered in a Chinese restaurant, Alice always says something that has to do with duck. "You know, this place seems like the kind of place that would have great duck," she'll say, apparently having figured that out from the shade of formica on the table tops. I don't mean to complain: our friend William Edgett Smith, the man with the Naugahyde palate, always says something like, "You know, this place seems like the kind of place that would have great egg foo-

yung." I do like duck. I particularly liked Herman
Perrodin's duck. It was by far the best thing on the
plate — moist on the inside and crisp on the outside,
with no fat in sight. I suppose I might have found the
duck particularly satisfying because I realized that, as
a member of the general public, I might be having my
last shot at it.

ॐ

As soon as I arrived in Opelousas, I was assured that
the New York miniconglomerate had signed the wrong
man. "They didn't do enough research before they
closed the deal," one of the breakfast regulars at the
Palace Cafe, on the courthouse square, explained to
me. In Opelousas, the Perrodins' Baton Rouge version
of Didee's was barely acknowledged ("I think they
started some kind of catering service over in Baton
Rouge"). From the way Baton Rouge was discussed at
the Palace, I got the idea that anybody in Opelousas
who has business in the capital waits until he gets
back home to eat. Baton Rouge was described as a
place where the state government and the petro-
chemical industry have drawn so many people from
places like north Louisiana or even Mississippi that
there might not be a tableful of eaters in the entire
city who know the difference between splendidly prepared duck and the kind of fowl that might be considered edible by Baptists. Herman Perrodin could
hardly have learned the secrets of baked-duck cooking

from Didee as a boy, I was told by a man who had delivered milk to the restaurant for many years, since Didee was accustomed to sitting out on the sidewalk whittling while his wife did the cooking. The dairyman said Herman would not have been around the restaurant much anyway; even as a boy, he was apparently what people in Opelousas call "kinda sporty."

As if that were not complication enough, some lawyer in Opelousas who once had some business with Thomas Blouin, the proprietor of Dee Dee's while it lasted, informed me that Blouin had recently come off the oil rigs to take a job cooking at a restaurant between Opelousas and Lafayette, where he was prepared to cook the true Opelousas stupefying baked-duck dinner for me and most of the law firm of Sandoz, Sandoz & Schiff. At the restaurant, a place called Carroll's, near Evangeline Downs race track, I was pleased to find that Sandoz, Sandoz & Schiff lawyers are the sort of lawyers who find it easier to get down to cases if they have a pile of boiled crawfish to work on while they talk. What they talked about mainly was food. "Her oyster loaf was a knockout," one of the lawyers said, recalling how Miz Anna would scoop the middle out of a perfect French loaf and replace it with succulent fried oysters. That reminded another member of the firm about stopping in after work with a large pot he kept in his car and having Miz Anna fill it with seafood gumbo before he went home. As they talked, the lawyers deftly peeled crawfish and popped them into their mouths. It occurred to me that if a society of sausage fanciers was ever founded, the firm of Sandoz, Sandoz & Schiff might be a good bet for general counsel. "If it please the court," the firm's litigation partner would say in our defense, "I would ask that the term 'food crazy' used by this witness be stricken from the record." Conferences would be held in grocery-store parking lots, where the officers of the association and their attorneys could lean up against a Pontiac and chomp away at boudin. The bylaws drawn up by Sandoz, Sandoz & Schiff would make it clear that all association business would be suspended on those days when, as is sometimes said in southern Louisiana, "the crawfish are walking right across the highway."

About the time we had knocked off our first conversational bowl of crawfish, Thomas Blouin came out from the kitchen to sit down with us for a while before putting the finishing touches on the meal. He turned out to be a rather modest man, as southern Louisiana cooks go, although he did admit later in the evening that he could prepare wild duck, a notoriously difficult fowl to cook, so well that it tasted like lemon pie. As Blouin told me about his training under Miz Anna, first as a waiter and then as a cook, the lawyers said "See!" and "Listen to that!" and "He knows his onions!" When I asked who had the real Didee recipe for duck, Blouin said, "You're fixin' to eat the recipe." The duck was delicious, if not quite as crisp as Herman Perrodin's. The dirty rice — a sort of rice dressing made with chicken liver and chicken gizzard and onion and bell pepper and celery and garlic and spices and oil — was staggering, although I speak as someone who had to go to a franchise fried-chicken place to find a dirty rice he didn't like. When I accepted Blouin's kind offer of another bowl of rice, there were cheers at the table, and a couple of lawyers clapped Blouin on the back. "They signed the wrong man," one of them said. "What'd I tell you." I couldn't help but wonder whether Henry Steele Commager had ever found himself in a similar situation.

ह॰

"Why, I bet he learned more about cooking on the oil rigs than he knew when Miz Anna died," Perrodin said when I reported the Opelousas theory about who knew how to cook Didee's duck. I had arrived back in Baton Rouge in time for a late lunch. Perrodin tossed off a few more disparaging remarks about Blouin, and then sat down to tell me how maquechou, a sort of stewed-corn dish the Omni executives and I had been served at Didee's with lunch, was prepared by a cook who really knew how to get your whole mouth lit up.

"But will they be able to do that sort of thing at a Didee's franchise in Alexandria or Shreveport?" I asked after Perrodin had finished a five-minute speech that included pulling his tongue out now and then to show me which part of the mouth was affected by which flavor. "Aren't you afraid they'll take shortcuts with preparation and ingredients?"

Perrodin leaned way back in his chair and stared at me, as if to make certain I had not disappeared from dumbness. "That was *canned* corn you had in the maquechou," he said. "What I was just explaining to you was the authentic way to do it. Who the hell's got time to do that?"

Thinking back on the meal, I remembered that when one of the Omni executives mentioned his company's roll into real estate, it had occurred to me that Perrodin's dinner rolls had the look of packaged hamburger buns about them. "But how about the duck?" I asked. "Doesn't that take a lot of care and experience — all that time in your grandfather's kitchen learning the secrets?"

"There are no secrets," he said. "Any idiot could do it. Why, I could stay home and tell you how to do it over the phone, and I bet *dollars* it would come out the same."

He took a fork and poked around at the duck I was eating. "Shortcuts!" he said. "This duck was cooked last night. I reconstituted it by putting it back in natural sauce just to get it warmed through. When somebody orders it, I take it out of its natural gravy and put it under the salamander and let this overhead-broiler heat come down on it, and it brings it back just like I took it out of the oven."

As Perrodin expanded on the subject, shortcuts began to sound as dramatic as spectacular gumbo or a serious heroin habit. "Why, I can take almost any kind of canned vegetable and I'll defy you to tell me if it's fresh," he said. "Shortcuts! I'm the *master* of the shortcut. I mean to tell you."

Ordering in Japanese

ALL IN ALL, I spend a lot of time — time other people might spend worrying about their tax situation or the Bomb — worrying about the possibility that I might go right through a meal somewhere and still miss the good stuff. That's what worried me about going to Tokyo. How was somebody who couldn't seem to master a few wall signs in an American Chinatown going to figure out what the special of the day was in Tokyo? Talk about the Mysteries of the East! Even in European countries that are thoughtful enough to conduct their business in the Roman alphabet, I often get edgy during meals because of a suspicion that the regulars are enjoying some local specialty that the management has hidden from travelers by listing it on the menu in a foreign language. Once, while Alice and I were eating lunch in a Sicilian city called Piazza Armerina, I became nearly frantic at not being able to figure out what was meant by the special of the day listed as Bocca di Lupo — a dish my high-school Latin led me to believe was called Mouth of the Wolf. Before placing an order, I thought it prudent to confirm my assumption that the phrase was not meant literally, but no such dish was listed in the dictionary of menu terms that I keep with me at all times in a foreign country — the way some travelers always carry their passport and a carefully hidden American fifty-dollar bill. The waiter spoke no English, and he just looked puzzled when I, having quickly exhausted my Italian, cleared my throat and did what seemed to me a passable wolf imitation. We never did order the special of the day, and I have assumed ever since that it is only a matter of time before we run into some old Sicilian hand who says, "I hope you got to Piazza Armerina for some of that marvelous Bocca di Lupo."

I was thinking of Bocca di Lupo as Alice and I flew over the Pacific on the way to our first stay in Tokyo. I like the Japanese food served in New York, even though I have sometimes heard Alice discuss the purity of Japanese ingredients — the sort of talk that can ordinarily put me off my feed. What was to be found in Tokyo would presumably be even better, but how were we meant to find it? "How am I going to get along in a place as foreign as Japan when even an Italian menu can cause me to bay in a public place?" I asked Alice.

"Where's your spirit of adventure?" Alice said. She reminded me what I had said about pushing out frontiers in the interest of pure research — and conveniently forgot that she had not been eager to take a flyer on Bocca di Lupo herself.

I settled down to my airplane reading — a book that displayed colored pictures of Japanese dishes and explained what they were. "The word for noodles is 'udon,'" I announced right away. I always take the precaution of learning the word for noodles before entering any country, just in case. "Unless you want the polite form," I went on, "which is 'o-udon.' That's what I mean about mystery: why would anyone want to be anything but polite about noodles?"

My precaution turned out to be well taken. "O-udon!" I was able to shout, politely, during a stroll on our very first morning in Tokyo, as I stopped Alice in her tracks and pointed to a store window beyond which someone was rolling out noodle dough. By then, I was already feeling much less concerned about the possibility that the language barrier could lead to my starvation. Having arrived in Tokyo the previous evening tired from the flight, we had gone no further for dinner than the hotel's sushi restaurant — where it became apparent that someone sitting at a sushi bar, rather than at a table, can get his fill simply by pointing at the fish on display. Sitting at the bar is the best place to eat sushi anyway, since a good sushi chef puts on a good show — responding to any order with an almost military "Hai!", a couple of taps with his knife to get the rhythm, some quick strokes at the raw fish, an abrupt jab to plant the fish in a ball of rice, and a flick of the wrist as he places the finished product on the bar in front of you. According to a pocket-size sushi-identification chart we picked up on the way in, we managed, without saying a word, to eat tuna, belly of tuna (I thought I might like a country that troubles to distinguish among cuts of tuna), abalone, salmon roe, sea urchin, "interior of arch shell," and, finally, some mysterious but fantastic mixture of fish and herbs that we ordered by displaying enthusiasm as it was being prepared for someone else.

"Aji no tataki," I had said the next morning, after a long session with my food-picture book.

"Does that mean 'I ate too much' in Japanese?" Alice asked.

"It's what we had last night at the end of the meal," I said. I read from the text: "'Small pieces of pompano chopped and mixed with onions, ginger, and sometimes leeks.'" My confidence was growing, and it wasn't depleted by noticing that other sources identified aji as horse mackerel or a type of herring. I felt that I had broken the code.

By the time we stood in front of the store window admiring the technique of the noodle maker, it had also become apparent that we had another great demystification device at our disposal — the Japanese custom of restaurants displaying in their windows full-size, absolutely realistic models of whatever dishes they're offering. We had spent the morning wandering around Asakasa, a neighborhood of small shops and a serious temple and a pleasant little amusement park where I had lost badly in hand-wrestling to a mechanical suma wrestler, and a lot of what we had paused to admire had been models of sushi and sashimi and tempura and noodles and lightly fried fish — my idea of window-shopping. When we reached the noodle shop, I realized that I was famished. One of the models it displayed looked particularly tempting — a large bowlful of soup with thick white noodles and two huge mushrooms and a bean-curd cake. We marched into the restaurant — a small, immaculate place — and I beckoned the proprietor to come with me. He was polite but hesitant. Did he think that I may have once suffered some slight at his hands which he had long ago forgotten and was now, as they say in the saloons, inviting him to step outside? Had some recent article comparing Japanese and American crime statistics put him on his guard to the point where he suspected that going outside with me might give Alice a shot at the cash register? Could he possibly have mistaken me for some sort of exchange-program public-health inspector who might object to noodles being made in the window? I could reassure him on that point by informing him that, quite the contrary, I had once offered to establish a defense fund for a barbecue man on the west coast of Florida who had allegedly assaulted a public-health inspector for suggesting that he clean his grill more than once a year — except that I don't know how to reassure in Japanese.

Whatever misgivings the noodle-shop proprietor had, though, were overcome by his courtesy. He stepped outside. We studied the window together. As I tried to indicate what I wanted, I realized that my menu dictionary was remiss in offering me translations only for words like "grilled" and "well done." What I needed to know how to say in Japanese was "No, not that one — the one just behind it, near the corner." In a moment, though, he gave a quick nod, we went back inside, and a waitress brought to the table a precise replica of the replica. It was delicious. It cost the equivalent of two dollars.

"No wonder the crime rate is so low in Japan," I said to Alice. "Everybody must be very, very happy."

"Tako yaki," I said to Alice, as we stood in front of a street vender and watched him pour batter into the rows of half-circle indentations of an iron griddle — like one of those college kids at Williamsburg demonstrating how musket balls were made. "It's listed right here in the book under Street and Festival Foods." What we were attending was not a festival but an astonishing ritual that happens with enough regularity to draw a few dozen street venders. Every Sunday afternoon, a boulevard near the Olympic stadium becomes filled with thousands of Japanese teenagers who arrive in groups of a dozen or so, the members of each group dressed identically in costumes of the fifties. Each group gathers in a circle around a huge tape recorder that is playing songs like "Rock Around the Clock"

and "Let's Go to the Hop," dances a carefully choreo-graphed version of the twist in unison, and somehow seems very Japanese doing it. Naturally, I tried a tako yaki, but then I discovered a problem with eating completely foreign foods which I hadn't anticipated: was it possible that I didn't like tako yaki or had I stumbled across the one tako yaki stand that knowing tako-yaki eaters always avoid? I had to have several versions of tako yaki to settle that question — as it turns out, I don't like tako yaki — but then I fell into the same trap with four or five other street foods. By the time I could announce with certainty that I liked the fried buckwheat noodles being sold at half a dozen stands, I felt I had rocked several times around the clock. "There's no substitute for an adequate sample," I said to Alice.

My confidence continued to grow. At a sushi bar near the central fish market, I realized that I did not have to remain silent when I pointed at a delectable-looking piece of tuna. I could point and say anything I wanted to — "Tippecanoe and Tyler too" or, *"Où se trouve la plage?"* The results were the same. "Hai!" the sushi chef would bark, and tap his knife a couple of times on the cutting board in anticipation. All sorts of Japanese restaurants tend to display their food, so we found that at, say, a yaki-tori restaurant — a restaurant that specializes in grilling various parts of a chicken and various vegetables over charcoal — we could get whatever we wanted grilled by simply pointing to it and saying *"Semper fidelis"* or "You wanna buy a duck?"

Also, we discovered the food halls of the department stores. All of the large department stores devote their bottom floor or two to food — not just packaged food but fish and produce and salads and pastry and just about anything else anybody could think of to eat. Not only that — they give samples. "I can't believe it," I said to Alice, as we walked through the ground floor of a department store on the Ginza, politely trying out the shrimps and the dumplings and the salmon and the rice cakes. "It's a Japanese bar mitzvah. A person could have lunch here."

"I think you just did," Alice said.

I would maintain that I had not actually eaten lunch — I offer as proof the fact that just a few minutes later I ate lunch at a little yaki-tori place called Torigin, around the corner — but Alice may have been right in remarking that I had attracted the attention of some salesclerks. If I lived in Tokyo, I suppose that could get to be a problem: I can imagine the clerks whispering to each other as I walked off the escalator around the middle of some pleasant weekday, "He's here — the foreign one who eats." They would snatch their toothpicks off the sample tables. An assistant manager would approach me, smiling broadly, and lead me firmly toward the elevator, with a grip like a mechanical suma wrestler. Smiling, he would say, "How nice to see you again. Perhaps you would like to visit our fine selection of notions and gifts on the fifth floor."

Of course, some mysteries remained unsolved. On a trip
to Kyoto, we went directly from a traditional breakfast
at a Japanese inn to the garden of the Ryonaji Temple,
a garden whose simple perfection inspires people to
contemplate all sorts of profundities as they gaze upon
it, and all I could think of as we stood there was "What
could that orange thing next to the fish possibly have
been?" Of course, errors were made. Occasionally, we
would point to something being greatly enjoyed by
some diners a few tables away only to find when it
arrived that it fell in that category of small sea
creatures and odd weeds that a longtime Tokyo resident named Ellen Reingold has summed up evocatively
as "low-tide stuff."

Usually, though, a mistake did not mean disaster.
On the morning I visited the central fish market, for
instance, I made a mistake while ordering my third
breakfast. My first two breakfasts had gone off without a hitch. I had started eating at about seven-thirty,
with some very good noodles in broth. By then, I had
spent a couple of hours wandering around the market,
a place I found almost as astounding as the boulevard
of dancing teenagers. In what seemed to be acres of
market-shed, thousands of fish were arranged with
military precision for inspection by the people who
would bid for them. Most of the fish were displayed in
neat stacks of white Styrofoam boxes — so that, depending on size, a box might contain one mackerel or
twenty-four perfectly aligned smelts. The huge tuna
were lined up outside in precise rows, with a steak-size

flap pulled back on each fish for inspection of the meat. The place was so clean and the fish so fresh that I suppose it might have struck some people as a confirmation of the purity of Japanese ingredients, but it just made me hungry.

After my noodle breakfast and a sushi breakfast, I pressed my face against the window of a tiny lunch counter where the short-order man started what seemed to be an onion stew in a frying pan, dropped what I took to be a breaded halibut steak into a deep-fat fryer, switched the steak to the frying pan after a while, broke an egg on top, and then put a cover on the frying pan to let the whole concoction cook together. It looked so good that I went in pointing. The halibut steak turned out to taste a lot like a pork cutlet. Tongetsu! After some consultation with my portable research library, I finally realized I was eating a version of tongetsu — a pork dish popular in inexpensive Japanese restaurants. "And excellent tongetsu at that," I said, drawing some of the same sort of looks that I had provoked in Sicily with my wolf imitation. "My compliments to the chef."

The most serious problem was in restaurants that were too sophisticated to have food models in the window but too Japanese to have a menu in English. One evening, we wandered into a restaurant whose specialty seemed to be a fish stew that was cooked at the table — a sort of marine sukiyaki. Nobody spoke English. We went with the specialty — although I could see from observing some other diners that it was going to involve having someone hover around the table, picking bits out of the bubbling pot and encouraging us to eat. We had just had two straight meals like that — a constantly attended dinner at a Japanese inn followed by lunch at a fine sukiyaki place near the restaurant-supply area, where we had gone to buy some sushi models — and I was beginning to feel like a college freshman who arrives home late one night for his first Christmas vacation and is not allowed to go to sleep until he sits at the kitchen table eating some of his mother's specialties under the watchful eye of his mother ("You don't want any Swedish meatballs? You've always loved my Swedish meatballs. Here, have some Swedish meatballs"). Some of the fish in the pot looked very mysterious. Alice picked up a roundish lump with a black appendage on it, and peered at it suspiciously.

"A pure ingredient," I said helpfully.

She tried the black appendage.

"Shrewd of you to bite off the toe before you start on the body," I said.

Alice picked carefully at the remainder of the beast. "It's not bad," she said, "although I wish I knew what it was."

"Well, this is strictly a fish restaurant," I said. "Otherwise, I might conclude that we'd found, at long last, Mouth of the Wolf."

A Real Nice Clambake

ITHINK it's only prudent to be wary about accepting an invitation to attend a clambake at a gentlemen's club. I always thought of a clambake as a long picnic whose atmosphere is somewhere between informal and roistering — the sort of event that ends up late in the evening with bad sunburns and worse singing and a demand by the big fellow who has had too much beer that everyone help him display his strength by forming a pyramid on his stomach. Wouldn't a gentlemen's club version of that event result in a lot of sand getting down into the leather armchairs? My suspicion that a gentlemen's club might be an unusually formal setting for a clambake was confirmed by the person who had in fact phoned to invite me to a clambake at the Squantum club, in Providence — a newspaper reporter named Donald Breed. Breed hadn't been a member of the Squantum long, and he confessed that when he showed up for his

first clambake wearing a sport coat but no tie he was
drawn aside by the steward, who reminded him, in a
kindly sort of way, that he was not properly dressed
for the occasion. I had to confess that I was wary
about accepting an invitation to eat anything at a
gentlemen's club. Although I naturally deplore those
researchers who make unseemly efforts to elbow ahead
of their colleagues in publishing particularly flashy
findings, it happens to be a matter of record that I was
first in print with the discovery that the tastelessness
of the food offered in American clubs varies in direct
proportion to the exclusiveness of the club. After many
years of trying to ascertain the cause of this phe-
nomenon, I even came up with a rather persuasive
theory: the food in such places is so tasteless because
the members associate spices and garlic with just the
sort of people they're trying to keep out.

When I spoke to Breed on the telephone, I got the
impression that the Squantum club is, as men's clubs
go, fairly flexible about bloodlines — although not to
the point of retaining a chef who goes heavy on the
oregano and schmaltz. Breed told me that the Squantum
had actually been founded in the mid-nineteenth century by people who were drawn together by a strong
interest in eating seafood — it is built on a point that
juts into Narragansett Bay — and that it had never
strayed from the values of its founders to the extent
of installing anything like a golf course or a sauna
bath. Breed said that the Squantum bake could provide
a sort of warm-up for the first public bake of the

season at Francis Farm a few days later — Francis Farm, in Rehoboth, Massachusetts, not far from Providence, being a place that stages clambakes of the sort that last all day and include horseshoe pitching and may even feature, now and then, a big fellow who wants everyone to form a pyramid on his stomach. I told Breed that I would be pleased to join him at the Squantum, and he asked me — in the discreet way people ask, now that we have passed through an era in which anybody might show up anywhere wearing anything — if I happened to own a necktie.

Like a lot of serious shellfish eaters I have encountered over the years, Breed had a landlocked childhood — in northwestern Illinois, near the Wisconsin state line. He was fortunate enough to come to roost in a section of the Northeast where the custom of clambakes remains strong. People all over New England, of course, have always baked clams on the beach — built a fire of hardwood over stones that will retain the heat, then piled on four or five inches of rockweed that pops and sizzles as it steams — but the custom seems particularly institutionalized around Providence. Elderly people in the area speak of going by horse and buggy earlier in the century to annual clambakes that are still being held — the Hornbine Church Bake, for instance, or the Moosup Valley Grange Bake. There are said to be old-timers around Providence who can tell from the taste of a clam not just where it came from but whether it was baked over oak or cherry.

Around Narragansett Bay, in fact, the tradition of clambakes seems to have outlasted the clams. Although there are still enough quahogs in the bay for chowder, the clams that are actually baked on a clambake tend to be soft-shell clams trucked in from Maine. The Narragansett clam supply has been cut by pollution, of course, but some studies done at the University of Rhode Island indicate that an equally serious threat to the supply of clams and flounder and cod and tuna and the other seafoods traditionally eaten in this country is the rigidity of American notions about which fish is and which fish is not fit to eat. A project at U.R.I. has done what it could do for the popularity of such "underutilized species" as the ocean pout, a fish that looks almost as bad as it sounds, and the dogfish, which the Rhode Island specialists prefer to call the grayfish. One of the people involved, Spiros Constantinides, told me that the strain on the clam supply could be eased if people simply utilized the available mussels and whelks as well. If the University of Rhode Island folks had their way, high-school productions of *Carousel* would probably include a song entitled "This Was a Real Nice Whelk Bake."

I like mussels myself, and I think that over the years I have done my share to see that they are not underutilized. In Nova Scotia, I often feel exceedingly virtuous when the girls and I go to a place that everyone else uses as a clam flat and gather mussels instead —

and I feel even better when Alice transforms our haul into moules marinière. From Nova Scotia to Japan, I have done my level best to improve the reputation of the eel ("Not slimy at all. It's really not slimy. If I had to describe it in a word, 'slimy' is certainly not the word I'd use"). I suppose I would eat a whelk if anyone ever thought to offer me one. I regret that I cannot say the same for my daughters. I have spent so much time, mostly to no avail, trying to persuade Abigail and Sarah to utilize the overutilized species of fish that turning to the underutilized might seem like an act of folly. If talking Sarah into trying flounder required that much effort, what chance would I have with the ocean pout?

Virtuous as I am about downing mussels, I must still admit that I am partly responsible for the strain on the clam supply. I like clams. I like steamed clams and clams on the half shell — although the first time I saw one of those, when I was fresh from my own landlocked childhood, I assumed it was some sort of prank. I love fried clams. I like clam chowder so much that I have occasionally been willing to listen to Boston and New York fanciers argue about whether its base should be tomatoes or cream — the East Coast equivalent of the even drearier southwestern argument about what belongs in chili — as long as I had a bowl of one type or the other in front of me during the discussion. In fact, almost as soon as I sat down for dinner at the Squantum — in a huge outbuilding called a bakehouse, which the members had the good sense to build on a patch of ground that people lacking their historical perspective might have used for a tennis court — I realized how the chowder theorists might symbolize the identity problem facing Providence as the large northeastern coastal city that is neither Boston nor New York: some places around Providence, including the Squantum, make clam chowder with both cream and tomatoes, so that the bitter argument between red and white is avoided with an ambivalent pink.

The chowder had been preceded by clams on the half shell — served at the main clubhouse, a spectacular turn-of-the-century pile overlooking the bay — and clam broth and clam fritters. After some sausage and sweet potatoes and the baked clams themselves, the waitress brought around a dish of ice cream. I told Breed that the Squantum bake was a pretty good feed — considering that it was run by a gentlemen's club fancy enough to line up five forks at each place setting, and that many of those in attendance seemed of an age to exercise some moderation about what they ate in the six or eight hours before bedtime. Breed informed me that we were being served ice cream merely to cleanse the palate for the rest of the meal. Although I didn't remember any palate cleansing at the *Carousel* clambake, I followed the example of my host — and then followed it again as he downed some shad and a dish of coleslaw and more potatoes and a small lobster and some Indian pudding. The assembled club members consumed all this with routine dignity, as if they were eating prime ribs of beef au jus with potatoes au gratin and choice of one vegetable.

Breed was already talking about the bake to be held at Francis Farm a few days later. "Go easy on the clam cakes out there," he warned me.

"Aren't they any good?" I asked.

"Delicious," he said. "Small and very crisp. But they'll fill you up for the clams. You have to pace yourself."

"The chowder makes them expand in your stomach," one of the regulars at the Francis Farm public bake explained to me the following Sunday. He was warning me about the clam cakes, and he was popping some of them into his mouth as he gave the warning. I had brought the entire family to Francis Farm for the public bake, but I had also resigned myself to the fact that Abigail and Sarah were likely to be there as spectators rather than participants. Although I had assured them that they were not required to eat clams, Sarah was eyeing the fire with the sort of expression that might be seen on someone who had been told that it was being prepared for human sacrifices.

Like the Squantum, Francis Farm has been putting on clambakes for about a century, but, unlike the Squantum, where only the clams are actually baked over the traditional wood coals and seaweed, Francis Farm is militantly anti-stove. Except for the substitution of iron ingots for large stones, the bake at Francis

Farm is done the way it has always been done —
starting with a four-foot-high hardwood fire. As the
fire burns down, a troupe of college boys appears, like
travelogue natives who have always known their role
in the ritual. The coals and ingots are raked smooth,
bags of rockweed are piled on, a screen is placed over
the rockweed, just about everything anybody intends
to eat is placed on the screen, and the entire pile is
covered with canvases until the college boys return an
hour later to "pull the bake." Francis Farm uses the
traditional fire to bake clams, lobsters, sausage, filet of
pollack, onions, and even stuffing. George Taylor —
who, along with his father-in-law, Frank Miller, bought
the clambake operation from the Francis family in
1959 — likes to say that everything is done "on the
bake" except the chowder and the clam cakes, the
watermelon, the coffee, and the condiments.

Most of the clambakes staged at Francis Farm are
private — for a lodge gathering, say, or a company
picnic or a high-school reunion. The grounds are arranged like back-to-back summer camps — summer
camps where everyone is well fed and not homesick
and allowed to drink beer without worrying about being
spotted by a counselor — and there are two clambakes
a day every day of the summer. A lot of the organiza-
tions come back the same day every year; the Red
Man Lodge has thrown a clambake at Francis Farm on
the first Saturday in August for more than sixty years.
A true joiner, of course, can manage several cracks at
the clams every summer. A bank officer named Tom

Brady, for instance, told me he had come once that summer with the Rhode Island Commandery of the Military Order of Foreign Wars, once with the Sons of Irish Kings, and once with the bank he worked for. Apparently not having gotten his fill, he was back for a public bake.

Francis Farm holds nine public clambakes a summer — building up to a crowd of seven or eight hundred people by August — and even those bakes seem dominated by regulars. The man sitting across from me — Dick Lundgren, a sales engineer from Seekong, Massachusetts — said he had been going to bakes off and on for forty years, ever since, as a child, he accompanied his father to the annual bake of the Seekong Volunteer Fire Department. He told me that he attended most of the public bakes, and always sat at the same table with Len Estes, who ran boiler rooms for one enterprise or another before he retired in Newport, and Ed Gardner, a grounds keeper for the University of Rhode Island, in Kingston. The regulars called each other by their last names — perhaps because last names were written in marking pen on the paper tablecloth in front of each plate — and what they said tended to be something like "Pass the melted butter, Gardner" or "Are there any more clams over there, Estes?"

I was hungry, and I was feeling particularly virtuous, having dined the previous evening on broiled scup — a fish that sounds bad enough to be an underutilized species, although it happens to taste very good. For a while, I seemed to be keeping up with Lundgren and Estes and Gardner, and so did Alice. She got so interested in eating clams that she forgot to tell me that I shouldn't feel compelled to eat as many as one of the regulars. I got so interested that I neglected my efforts to persuade the girls that they might like some of the food — efforts based on the contention that the pollack tasted like flounder and the sausage tasted like hot dogs and the potatoes tasted like, well, potatoes. Abigail had a few spoonfuls of chowder, and then they wandered off toward the bake fire, apparently curious about whether a missionary might be thrown in after all.

Then I started to pace myself to leave room for the dishes Breed had recommended highly — the clams and the onions and the pollack. The regulars next to me continued to hand out their own pacing advice, ignoring it all the while. Down the table, Breed seemed to be eating everything indiscriminately. Next to him, Tom Brady was eating in his own clambake style — pouring melted butter into a coffee cup and then tossing everything into it, like a Chinese eater constantly adding to a bowl of rice. ("Not everything," Brady told me later, in the tone of someone accused of using the wrong fork. "I never put in the stuffing.")

When I commented on the steady eating, I was informed by the regulars that the most serious eater among them, a Boston maintenance man named Bastow, had not shown up. At the final bake of the previous season, Bastow had apparently mentioned that he would be changing jobs, and some of the regulars surmised that he was no longer able to get away on Sundays. It sounded as if Bastow needed all of a Sunday to make it to the clambake, since he was said to take a train from Boston to Providence, a bus to Rehoboth, and, unless someone stopped to pick him up, a hike of two or three miles from Route 44 to the farm. "He's very skinny," Lundgren told me, "but he always has four bowls of chowder."

"He always heaps the last bowl high and covers it with a plate so it stays warm while he starts in on the clam cakes," one of the regulars said. "Then he takes a little walk, and comes back and finishes it off."

We were on the baked clams ourselves at the time. The waitress returned regularly to fill the platters, and Estes complained regularly about finding too many broken shells without clams. I was finding Breed's recommendations well considered. A clambake clam tastes like a steamer enhanced by a slight smoky flavor — and the same flavor works particularly well with fish and onions. "He's more than six feet tall," Estes said, talking of Bastow again.

"Completely bald," Lundgren added as he reached for more clams. "Doesn't drive a car."

"Mostly shells here," Estes said, picking around at the bowl of clams. "This must be the bottom of the barrel."

The waitress brought more clams and more onions and more brown bread and more sweet potatoes and more white potatoes. "Yes, sir," someone said. "He can eat four bowls of chowder, then go to the bar for a beer."

"He's six-foot-six and thin as a rail," Estes said. "He must be about a foot wide." Estes turned to Gardner. "Wouldn't you say about a foot wide?"

"Yeah, about a foot," Gardner said between bites of pollack.

The regulars were still talking about Bastow as they finished off their watermelon. Suddenly, the meal was over, and they disappeared. A private clambake at Francis Farm usually lasts most of the day — there is ordinarily a break of a few hours for recreation between the clam-cake-and-chowder course and the time the bake is pulled — but some regulars at a public bake just show up to eat. I went to compliment George Taylor on the meal and to ask him if there really was a storied eater named Bastow.

"Oh, yeah — he looks like Silas Marner," said Taylor, who once was a high-school teacher. "I don't know what became of him today."

ॐ

I still think about Bastow, particularly when I'm hungry for clams. I can see his rising early in the morning in Boston, carefully straightening his small room, and silently setting out for the long journey to Rehoboth. "It's Bastow," one of his neighbors says to another. "Off again — wherever he goes." At South Station, he digs an old-fashioned coin purse out of his pocket and buys a round-trip ticket to Providence. He stares out of the window of the train, thinking of clam cakes. At the bus station in Providence, the ticket agent just nods, and punches out a round trip to Rehoboth. "Bon appétit," the agent says. Bastow nods silently. He walks in from Route 44 toward Francis Farm — a steady pace, surprisingly graceful for a man who is six feet six inches tall and only a foot wide. Someone picks him up for the last mile or so — a fan, who says, "Four bowls today, Bastow?" Bastow smiles. Then they are at Francis Farm. The bake has been on for half an hour. Puffs of smoke escaping from under the canvas carry the smell of clams and onions. It is time for the chowder. Bastow sits down to eat.

Tasting

I MET PAULA ROME through Leo Braudy, her cheese-steak adviser. Braudy, who grew up in Philadelphia, is a cheese-steak authority of some renown who teaches English at Johns Hopkins on the side. It almost goes without saying that he is my kind of scholar. He analyzes what he often calls "the classic Philadelphia cheese-steak" with the sort of thoroughness he presumably expects his graduate students to use in dissecting *Paradise Lost*. He offers an essay on the essential crustiness of the roll. He uses literary allusions to comment on the steak itself — its tenderness, its crucial thinness. He cites research gathered from South Philadelphia to Swarthmore in discussing the way the steak blends with the cheese and the cheese blends with the onions. He footnotes, with scholarly detachment that is compromised only by an almost imperceptible shudder, the preference of some cheese-steak eaters for mayonnaise rather than the traditional hint of ketchup. Although Braudy's friends speak of his knowledge of cheese-steaks as falling somewhere in that gray area between thorough and obsessive, he is hardly a one-subject scholar. He is also considered an authority on the Philadelphia hoagie. I have heard him compare the Philadelphia hoagie with what he considers the inferior foreign versions — submarines, grinders, heroes, po' boys. I have heard him compare one Philadelphia hoagie to another Philadelphia hoagie. I have even heard him compare Philadelphia hoagies to Philadelphia cheese-steaks — a critical tour de force that I believe a Hopkins graduate student might classify as "interdisciplinary."

When Braudy introduced me to Paula Rome, she had need of a cheese-steak adviser because she was employed as what amounted to a professional taster. She worked for the Rouse Company, which specializes in developing what it calls "marketplaces" — the best known of which is the collection of restored brick buildings on the Boston waterfront known as the Faneuil Hall Marketplace. Rouse had hired Paula Rome in connection with a similar project, called Harborplace, that it was then building on the inner harbor of Baltimore — the problem of Baltimore's lack of any old warehouses whose brick could be artistically exposed having been solved by beginning new buildings from scratch. One of them was due to contain almost nothing but food — a number of market stalls, a couple of full-service restaurants, and twenty-five fast-food booths. Mrs. Rome, whose experience included some restaurant reviewing in Baltimore, had been hired partly to help decide which twenty-five they should be. She had tasted the products of people who inquired about renting space. She had sniffed around the area for food discoveries — driving to Eldersburg, where she had a tip on a Mexican restaurant in a shopping center, for instance, or sampling the foodstuffs at a Frederick crafts fair, where she came upon a drink called Flying Fruit Fantasies. When I met her, she was involved in planning a bake-off among the nineteen separate enterprises that had approached Harborplace about a chocolate-chip-cookie stand. In other words, she had the job that a lot of people I know have been looking for.

I might as well admit that learning what Paula Rome did for a living set my own daydreams in the direction of professional tasting. I had already thought of myself as a devoted amateur. As I envisioned it, I would wander through the entire country looking for food to be included in a marketplace a block or so from my house — having easily solved the ostensibly insurmountable problems of geography and ingredients and logistics by reminding myself that it was all a fantasy anyway. In my thoughts, I spend a lot of time at Richard's, in Abbeville, Louisiana, carefully comparing their boiled crawfish and boiled shrimp to the fare served at the Guiding Star, in New Iberia. While I'm in the area, I do extensive boudin research, on the assumption that my design people will have no trouble simulating an authentic grocery-store parking lot. On the Lower East Side of Manhattan, I lean on the counter at Moishe's, chewing on a pumpernickel bagel while discussing how many square feet would be required for a good marketplace bagel operation. I sample oyster loaves in New Orleans and Italian-beef sandwiches in Chicago and smoked mullet on the west coast of Florida. I compare the Cuban sandwich served on the West Side of Manhattan with the Cuban sandwich served in Union City and the Cuban sandwich served in Miami and, if I can persuade Fidel Castro that my quest is not political but humanitarian, the Cuban sandwich served in Cuba. I toss around questions of policy. Could there be a french-fries booth that includes both french fries from Arthur Bryant's Barbecue in Kansas City — cooked in pure lard, with some of the skin left on here and there — and the pommes frittes served in a chic Santa Monica restaurant called Michael's? How about a booth that sells both the haute-cuisine version of calzone turned out by Alice Waters at Chez Panisse, in Berkeley, and plain old lower-Manhattan-Italian-feast four-pound calzone? Would wandering around a marketplace that is filled with food booths — a particularly festive marketplace — be the equivalent of attending the sort of festival at which a stand-up sausage sandwich might be eaten? I sit at Maurice's Snack 'n Chat, in Los Angeles, sampling the spoon bread and discussing with Maurice, the proprietress, the question of whether the proper marketplace name for it would be spoon bread or soufflé de maïs extraordinaire. I start to tell Maurice about my

plans to have a gelati stand and a stand selling aran-
cine, those little fried rice balls they sell on the street
in Sicily, but I have to cut the conversation short because I am on my way to the Zacatecas Café, in River-
side, to inquire about whether their Friday special of
nopales — cactus and cracklings — could be turned
into their Saturday-through-Thursday specialty as well.
Then I am back at Bryant's Barbecue in Kansas City,
in my professional capacity, trying to determine
through carefully controlled testing whether Bryant's
brisket would be suitable even for a marketplace
shopper who insisted on eating four or five pounds of
it at a sitting.

I had assumed that the central pleasure of being a
taster in Baltimore would come from eating crabs on
the job. The sort of crabs served at a traditional Baltimore crab house — done in a peppery crab boil, served
on butcher paper, and accompanied by a small mallet
— would be included in the marketplace of my dreams.
Unfortunately for Paula Rome, there had been no
further need for boiled-crab tasting by the time she
joined the organization, a deal having already been
made with Philips Crab House of Ocean City for one
of the full-service restaurants in the food pavilion. She
was, therefore, off duty when she and her husband and
Leo Braudy and his wife and I spent a long evening at
Gunning's, a crab house in south Baltimore, eating a
platterful of fifteens (crabs are customarily ordered
by how much they cost a dozen), accompanied by beer
and crab cakes and crab fluffs and soft-shell-crab sand-

wiches and coleslaw and french-fried onion rings and french-fried green-pepper rings. Braudy said that Gunning's was the only place he had been able to find green-pepper rings, even though he had spent a lot of time exploring the crab houses of the area — apparently in an effort to dispel the widespread notion that the perimeters of his gustatory interests could be defined by the city limits of Philadelphia. In my own marketplace, the response to that news would be straightforward: If Philips does not, in fact, serve equivalent french-fried green-pepper rings, it will simply have to expand its repertoire or make way for Gunning's.

Mrs. Rome made it clear that real-life tasting is not all that simple. For instance, she said, it was conceivable that a cheese-steak praised by Braudy as nearly adequate would not be appropriate for Harborplace for a variety of reasons that had nothing at all to do with its taste. In a project like Harborplace, agents have to consider which cheese-steak man got there first and which cheese-steak man helps the project's ethnic or racial balance and which cheese-steak man seems most capable of running an operation that can pay the rent and provide the sort of gross that the management, which gets a percentage of it, finds appealing. Deciding among nineteen chocolate-chip cookies might be the sort of task that fantasy tasters love to think about, but the final selection in a real project has to be made not just on how the cookie tastes but on how many of them can be produced how quickly — a fact brought home to Mrs. Rome when the cookie flogger at Faneuil Hall Marketplace told her that he was turning out forty to sixty thousand cookies a day.

Mrs. Rome acknowledged that in the eight months she had served as a professional taster she had tasted a lot of good food in the line of duty, but she had also eaten a lot of food that she might have politely declined outside business hours. "For the first few weeks," she told me, "all the food seemed to be brown." When I met Paula Rome, she had, as a professional taster, sampled Chinese and Japanese and Polish dumplings, chopped barbecued pork, barbecused sausage, barbecued ribs, knockwurst, bratwurst, bauernwurst, a wurst whose name she didn't catch, moussaka, stifado, cheese pie, spinach pie, golumbkas (stuffed cabbage), pirogen, a meatball submarine, a hamburger submarine, a chopped-beef-and-cheese submarine, many cheesesteaks (none of which, in Leo Braudy's view, cried out for comparison with a Shakespeare sonnet), many hoagies, a roast-beef sandwich, several corned-beef sandwiches, a gyro sandwich, a sausage sandwich with onions and peppers, a sprout-and-alfalfa sandwich with cucumbers and mushrooms, many hamburgers, a Boursin-and-bacon burger, eleven varieties of fried chicken, kang-pao chicken, tandoori chicken, champagne chicken, twenty-five Buffalo chicken wings with celery and blue-cheese dressing (in her office, at ten-thirty in the morning, only a couple of hours after Judy Katz would have polished off some Santora's leftovers for breakfast), french-fried potatoes, cheese french fries (created by somebody's accidentally spilling cheese on the french-fried potatoes at a place called Brothers' Steak-n-Take), western fries, baked potato stuffed with spinach and cheese, baked potato stuffed with sausage and vegetables, noodles with vegetables, tempura-fried vegetables, vegetable quiche, vegetable egg rolls, pork egg rolls, spring rolls, falafel, tabbouleh, tamales, fried dough, calzone, pâté, chopped liver, knishes, matzo balls, bagels, pizza bagels, pizza, midget pizza, Sicilian pizza, deep-dish pizza, Greek pizza, Mexican pizza, an enchilada and a burrito and a burrito supreme and several bowls of chili (all during the brown period), spinach with crab, crab soup, crab cakes, fried crab, fried oysters, seafood bisque, tofu-and-ginger seafood, fried fish, tandoori fish, avocado stuffed with shrimp, shrimp salad, tuna salad, a muffin stuffed with tuna salad (creating what its inventor called a muffit), a spinach muffit, a boeuf-bourguignon muffit, a ham-and-cheese muffit, a ham-and-cheese crêpe, a frittata, onion soup, zucchini soup, beet borscht, souvlaki, tandoori lamb, Hunan beef, moo-shu pork, Japanese-style steak, Polish sausage, beef kabob, baked ham, sautéed goat, duck stew, peanut stew on rice, sweet-potato greens on rice, stewed beef and rice, rice and beans, rice balls, broccoli-mushroom-and-cheese casserole, macaroni and cheese, fried eggplant, sorrel punch, lemon soda, lemonade, lemon cream, lemon chicken, turkey salad, salad niçoise, Greek salad, Greek bread, French bread, Indian bread, rye bread, pumpkin bread, fruit toast, pain de raisin, brioches, croissants, blueberry muffins, banana-nut muffins, apple-spice muffins, strawberry muffins, strudel in five varieties, a rum bun, a sweet-potato square, baklava, assorted Polish pastry, assorted Filipino pastry, gingerbread loaf, carrot cake, banana cake, apple-caramel cake, an unnamed cake with green icing, strawberry cake, cheesecake, amaretto cheesecake, chocolate cake, butter-cinnamon cake, almond cake, dessert burrito filled with apples, walnut-honey pie, peanut-butter oritani squares, Grand Marnier crêpe, miniature doughnuts, full-size doughnuts, full-size honey-dipped doughnuts, zeppole, brownies, pear tart, oatmeal cookies, Italian butter cookies, chocolate-topped cookies, raspberry sherbet, grapefruit sherbet, rum-raisin ice cream with fudge sauce, chocolate ice cream with fudge sauce, Oreo ice cream with fudge sauce, peanut-butter ice cream with fudge sauce, coffee-brickle ice cream with fudge sauce, orange-chocolate ice cream with fudge sauce, five varieties of fudge ("I like fudge actually; it's not a hardship"), tutti-frutti ice cream without fudge sauce, chocolate frozen yogurt, five varieties of soft pretzels, homemade potato chips, caramel corn, cheese corn, chocolate-dipped glacé fruit, chocolate-covered ginger, orange-chocolate wafers, coffee candies, rum cashew crispies, jelly beans, saltwater taffy, chocolate-covered banana-flavored saltwater taffy on a stick, and a lot of Tab — not to mention the nineteen varieties of chocolate-chip cookies. She had gained nine pounds.

I was not surprised to hear that nineteen people had inquired about setting up the chocolate-chip-cookie operation in Harborplace. When I wandered through

the Lexington Market in Baltimore — an old-fashioned
city market that no one would ever think of calling a
marketplace — I noticed that it had, among stalls
advertising chitterlings and hog maws and cut-up
chickens and pickles, a booth called Chippity-Doo-Dah.
The chippers were obviously thick on the ground. I was
surprised, though, to hear that the second-most inquiries had been received from purveyors of stuffed
baked potatoes — seven outfits with names like Meal-
in-a-Peel. My surprise was based partly on the fact that
I had been completely unaware that the baked potato
had become, as the saying goes, a meal in itself. I
realized what must have happened. There was a time
when Americans were accustomed to splitting their
baked potatoes and inserting a wedge of butter. Then
someone thought of sour cream. Then sour cream and
chives. Then bacon bits. For some years, that seemed
to be the extent of the potato-stuffing game. Then,
without my knowledge, someone apparently broke the
bacon-bit barrier. Mushroom sauce. Tuna fish. Sausage
and onion. Suddenly, there were no limits: chicken à la
king and jello mold could be seen on the horizon. Fast
food is fast. It is so fast, in fact, that Paula Rome had
to concern herself with the possibility that even before
Harborplace opened, the stuffed-potato game might
proliferate into the ubiquitous franchise operations
that the project was trying hard to avoid. The problems
facing a professional taster are enough to put a devoted
amateur off his feed.

Even before Paula Rome explained some of the complications of her job, though, my daydreams had started to take a dispiriting turn toward reality. In my thoughts, the design coordinator of the marketplace walked in, wearing designer blue jeans, and informed me that the folks at Richard's had refused to clear off crawfish shells in color-coordinated buckets instead of the galvanized ones they are accustomed to using — and that they might have replied to his request in an insulting manner, although their accent made it difficult for him to be certain. The security man informed me that it would be absolutely out of the question for Arthur Bryant to tend his barbecue pit all night, and that stacking hickory wood in front of the kite store "blocked egress." A delegation from an organization called Friends of the Desert began picketing the marketplace, claiming that the Zacatecas nopales "would inevitably lead to clear-cutting of cactus." The proprietor of Moishe's was threatening to pull out if Richard's did not agree to stop serving anything as overtly non-kosher as shellfish. Maurice, who had served three of the 257 customers lined up for her spoon bread, was complaining that turning out spoon bread at such a madcap rate might endanger quality. I walked back to her booth with her, hung out a sign saying "Closed Due to Harassment," asked for an order of spoon bread, and told her to take her time.

Fried-Chicken War

I SUPPOSE I ROMANTICIZED the fried-chicken
war of Crawford County a bit. When it comes
to fried chicken, I often get carried away. Word
of a dispute between Chicken Annie's and Chicken
Mary's, two regionally renowned fried-chicken em-
poriums in southeast Kansas, had reached me in New
York, where fried-chicken deprivation can cause someone who was raised in the Midwest to go feverish with
poultry nostalgia. In that condition, I took it for
granted that the hostilities in Crawford County —
hostilities that broke out when Chicken Annie's tried to
have the county road that runs in front of both estab-
lishments named Chicken Annie's Road — would engage fried-chicken devotees from several counties in
fearsome debate, characterized by completely bogus
historical references and sneering remarks about the
opposition's tendency to serve dried-out white meat. In
my own home town of Kansas City, after all, a peri-

patetic fried-chicken cook called Chicken Betty, who became well known some years after I had resigned myself to an Eastern life lacking in wishbones, inspired such fierce loyalty that droves of chicken eaters slavishly followed her from restaurant to restaurant, the way rich ladies might flock after a temperamental but brilliant hairdresser. On one trip home, I had caught up with Chicken Betty at a place called R.C.'s, in an annexed patch of the county people still call Martin City, and from that experience I knew that a movement to name a road after her would find me strongly opposed: whatever was named after Chicken Betty would have to be much more important than a road. Her fried chicken livers alone would merit a turnpike, and they're just a side dish. I would have long ago suggested that the airport be named after her — it still labors under the unfortunate and rather fanciful name of Kansas City International — if I hadn't been planning a campaign to have it named after Arthur Bryant, the city's premier barbecue man.

I realize that southeast Kansas is not the sort of place that strikes absolutely everybody as a dramatic setting. Kansas in general is not prime territory for a truly venomous conflict; folks try to get along. A lot of Crawford County looks like the peaceful Kansas where Dorothy and Aunt Em and Uncle Henry lived so contentedly before the cyclone hit, but the eastern part of the county, where Chicken Annie's and Chicken Mary's dispense their fried chicken, does have some of the elements that make for Old-World Drama. The settlement that set the tone for life in the southeast corner of Kansas — the section jammed in next to Missouri and Oklahoma, not far from Arkansas — was not a mid-nineteenth-century settlement of Ohio farmers looking for homestead land but an early-twentieth-century settlement of Europeans looking for work in the coal mines. A lot of people in eastern Crawford County are children or grandchildren of people who came to Kansas straight from Sicily or Austria or Bohemia. Years ago, the area acquired a reputation for tumultuous politics and reliable home brew. It is still sometimes called the Little Balkans.

Annie Pichler, who became known as Chicken Annie through her skill in that most American of specialties, was born in a small village not far from Budapest. She began selling fried chicken — cooked in her own kitchen, in a big iron skillet — because her husband got hurt in the mines and she had three children to raise. That was in 1934, in a place called Thirteen Camp — the coal camp next to the No. 13 mine of the Western Coal Company. Working through the Depression, in a poor corner of Kansas where most of the deep mines were already played out, Anne Pichler gradually made a name for herself — although she resisted the name Chicken Annie for a while because she thought it sounded "kind of raw." Then, in 1943, Mary Zerngast, whose husband had also had to give up work in the mines, opened a restaurant right where customers turned off the county road to get to Chicken Annie's. She served fried-chicken dinners. Mary Zerngast died in the late seventies, but when I went to Crawford County to investigate the chicken war I found Annie Pichler alive and well — a bouncy, friendly woman in her eighties — and though she told me "I don't want to hold grudges to anyone," she left no doubt in my mind about which family might be the object of any grudges she permitted herself. "They used to come and eat all the time, and then all of a sudden they went ahead and built on the county road right at the corner, blocking the way," she told me the day I got to Crawford County. "They got me a little upset." A feud! A European feud! By Kansas standards, an ancient European feud! I was not unmindful of what happened some years ago in the other Balkans because of a feud that did not even concern fried chicken: the First World War.

ૐ

By the time Chicken Annie's had moved into a new building out on the county road, in 1972, there wasn't much left of Thirteen Camp except the two fried-chicken restaurants, just a few hundred yards apart. Customers — as many as twelve hundred people at each place on a pleasant Saturday evening in the summer — drive in from somewhere else, and each restaurant has always tried to attract their attention by reaching around the competition with strategically placed signs. I figured that over the years, on some of those dark Balkan nights, signs for one place or the other might have blown over even when there wasn't much wind. "Oh, there was conflicts," Chicken Annie's daughter told me. "There was lots of conflicts."

The man who became proprietor of Chicken Annie's after Anne Pichler's retirement — her son-in-law, Louis Lipoglav — was convinced that most of Chicken Mary's customers were confused souls who thought they were at Chicken Annie's. The way Lipoglav figured it, hungry folks driving out from Pittsburg or Fort Scott or Coffeyville or Parsons could turn onto the county road from Highway 69 and stop at the first chicken restaurant they came to, even though he had attempted to clear up the confusion with a billboard at the turn and a huge sign next to Chicken Mary's parking lot informing chicken eaters that they only had to go another few hundred yards to reach the real article. When Lipoglav repainted his billboard one spring, he included a name for the road travelers were directed down — Chicken Annie's Road. Not long after that, without the matter's having gone before the county commission, an official county sign identified the road as Chicken Annie's Road for a couple of days — under circumstances about which both the Pichler-Lipoglavs and the Zerngasts were vague when I brought the subject up. Louis Lipoglav said, "Someone with the county put it up." Elizabeth Zerngast, Chicken Mary's daughter-in-law, said, "Someone tore it down.

After a decent interval, Lipoglav suggested that the county commission honor Anne Pichler by officially naming the road Chicken Annie's Road. The measure

was introduced by Joe Saia, who had been on the commission since 1939 and whose experience in such
matters extended to having had an entire overpass
named after him. Elizabeth Zerngast complained that
the name would advertise Lipoglav's restaurant rather
than honor Mrs. Pichler, the commission tabled the
matter, the local papers reported the outbreak of the
chicken war, and I, deciding that authentic combat
coverage demanded my presence on the scene, flew
from the East to Crawford County, chickens dancing
on pan-fried drumsticks in my head.

ॐ

"We have never fought, really," Elizabeth Zerngast
told me, as I sat in Chicken Mary's that afternoon. "It's
more kind of like little digs all the time. Like good
competitors. Competition kind of keeps you on your
toes." Even though she had objected to naming the
road in a way that would advertise her competitor,
Elizabeth Zerngast told me, she had no objection at all
to naming it Anne Pichler Road. "I know Anne Pichler
and I like her," Mrs. Zerngast said.

"You do?" It occurred to me that the Pichler-Lipoglavs
had also assured me that they had nothing personal
against the Zerngasts, even as they mentioned some
incidents that would try folks with less forgiving
natures. Even more surprising, both families assured
me that they had been pleased by the marriage some
year before of Chicken Annie's grandson and Chicken

Mary's granddaughter, who opened up a fried-chicken restaurant of their own just south of Pittsburg. It was as if the reaction of the Montagues and the Capulets to the romance of Romeo and Juliet had been to throw the young couple a big wedding bash and serve fried chicken. ("I prepared it, and they cooked it over at Chicken Annie's," Elizabeth Zerngast told me. "We had a real shindig.") Kansas people do tend to let bygones be bygones, but that's not an attitude I had associated with small villages near Budapest. Was it possible that the sun and the wind of rural Kansas caused European characteristics to evaporate faster than they might in a crowded northeastern city? I had noticed that the only restaurant in Frontenac, a heavily Italian town just north of Pittsburg, specialized in steak and — what else? — fried chicken. Was it possible that I was witnessing the de-Balkanizing of Crawford County?

ತ⋙

But where were the loyalists? I had assumed that the Crawford County fried-chicken war would include dramatic skirmishes between the Chicken Annie fancy and those who attended at Chicken Mary's. In Kansas City, where Arthur Bryant has an estimable rival in class barbecuing named Ollie Gates, I would take it for granted that a move to have the airport named after Bryant would face some resistance from hard-core Gatesites. During the Carter Administration, the Gates faction tried, unsuccessfully, to stop a proposed presidential visit to Bryant's by claiming that Mr. Bryant was a Republican — an accusation I discounted on the theory that Arthur Bryant has always been above politics. Could it be that there were no such loyalties in southeast Kansas? When I telephoned a serious eater I know in Fort Scott named Tom Eblen — a man who spent some years in Kansas City, most of them at Arthur Bryant's — he offered to meet me in Crawford County at either fried-chicken restaurant. This from a Bryantist who would no more suggest meeting at Gates's than he would suggest skipping lunch. If Eblen wasn't a loyalist, I figured, there couldn't be many loyalists.

As it turned out, some people eat only at Chicken Annie's or only at Chicken Mary's, but most people seem to patronize the two almost interchangeably. Even Commissioner Joe Saia, who is particular enough about food to turn out his own Sicilian salami, goes to both places, although he tends to speak of Annie's chicken as the standard he uses in rating the chicken he eats around the country at political conventions ("Colonel Sanders can't hold a light to it, and I've eaten a lot of the Colonel's, because he was a Democrat"). After eating at both places, I thought I understood the reason for the eerie tolerance people in the area show on the subject of fried chicken: although both Chicken Annie and Chicken Mary started out pan-frying chickens in huge iron skillets, they eventually turned to deep fryers. "People tell me it ain't the same," Chicken Annie told me, but nobody can pan-fry chicken fast enough to feed twelve hundred people a night. With a complete fried-chicken dinner for four people going for only about ten dollars, the Crawford County restaurants depend on volume. Chicken Annie's and Chicken Mary's do a good job of deep-frying chicken — they apply a non-Midwestern dose of garlic and they avoid the characteristic franchise batter that Chicken Betty has occasionally compared to a plaster cast — but a fried-chicken cook with a deep fryer is a sculptor working with mittens. I understood the practical, unromantic realities of running a large restaurant in a rural area that is not terribly prosperous, but the chickens that had danced in my head were dancing on pan-fried drumsticks. I decided that I might as well drop in on my home town, as long as I was so close. Although Chicken Betty had gone into semiretirement since my previous trip to Kansas City, I had heard that she was still presiding over the restaurant at the Metro Auto Auction, in Lee's Summit, on Tuesdays. The next day was Tuesday.

The Metro Auto Auction is strictly to the trade. It attracts dealers from all over the Midwest who want to beef up their used-car inventory. Wholesalers collect used cars from dealers, clean them up, and take them to Metro — "same as you buy a skinny cow, feed it out, and take it to slaughter," one dealer told me. The place does have the look of a cattle auction. On three lanes, distinguished according to the age of the cars being

sold, newly washed sedans and sports coupes and vans
pull up in front of the auctioneer. While the auctioneer
spews out his baffling chant — baffling, at least, to
anyone not in the trade — the buyers stand around
the cars being sold, occasionally peering under the
hood or circling warily to observe the paint job or
glancing in at the upholstery, until the auctioneer
finally says "Sold to Gary" or "Sold to Max." When the
buyers and sellers get hungry, they wander off the
selling floor into what seems like a little coffee shop —
a tiny place with a cafeteria line and no sign — and
there whatever sins they may have committed on the
used-car lot since the previous Tuesday are wondrously
forgiven. Without even leaving the building, they are
in the presence of Chicken Betty Lucas — the First
Lady of Fried Chicken, whose recipes have been
gathered for the *New York Times* by Mimi Sheraton,
and who in a just world would have a bridge (major
Missouri River crossing) named after her. There, on
the stove, are her iron skillets. Using the restraint one
learns in the East, I managed to wait until eleven
o'clock to have lunch.

The chickens dancing in my head had in fact been
chickens cooked by Chicken Betty — juicy chickens
with a light, peppery batter. Once I had reassured
myself on that point, I had a chat with Chicken Betty
— a cheerful, red-haired woman who still had the
no-nonsense manner of someone who had spent a
good deal of her life as a waitress. As a waitress or a
cook or a cashier or a bookkeeper, she moved when

she felt the need to ("Life's too short to work where you're unhappy") — trailing, toward the end of her career, throngs of chicken eaters in her wake. By the time she got to the Metro Auto Auction — semiretired and with a pacemaker helping her heart — she was allowing someone else to stand behind the iron skillets, but there remained no doubt about whose standards were in force. When the Metro Auto Auction asked Chicken Betty to do twenty-four hundred pieces of chicken for the celebration of its first anniversary in Lee's Summit, Chicken Betty told me, "My chef said, 'I guess with that many we'll have to drop them in a french-fryer,' and I said, 'No, we won't.'"

It occurred to me that Chicken Betty, with her purist attachment to the iron skillet, had not ended up with an empire. The little coffee shop at the Metro Auto Auction was really the only restaurant she had run rather than worked in since she became renowned — although she owned a bar many years ago, and for a while she and her husband ran a tavern called Eddie's Lounge. The years at Eddie's Lounge did not give Chicken Betty a taste for management; she often got fed up with the help — particularly with slovenly waitresses — and with her husband, who "mostly sat on the end bar stool." Betty Lucas grew up on a farm sort of like the one Aunt Em and Uncle Henry ran — it was in Nebraska rather than Kansas — and she acquired strong notions about doing any job right. "We are talking here about the last of the great pan-fryers," I figured I would tell the bridge-naming subcommittee of the City Council. "The empire builders in our midst are not interviewed respectfully by Mimi Sheraton."

I asked Chicken Betty whether she would do anything different if she had it to do all over again.

"If I was doing this all over?" Chicken Betty said, taking out her towel to wipe away a mark I couldn't see on the table. She smiled. "If I was doing this all over," she said, "I would have franchised."

A Few Beers
with Suds and Dregs

FOR SEVERAL YEARS, I had been looking for an opportunity to have a few beers with Suds Kroge and Dregs Donnigan, the authors of *A Beer Drinker's Guide to the Bars of Reading*. I like their style. It took a certain amount of flair, I always thought, for Suds and Dregs to spend a year investigating every single bar in Reading, Pennsylvania — a project that required stops at 132 bars, not counting return visits — and then dedicate the resulting book to their wives. I became familiar with *A Beer Drinker's Guide* when I ran across a copy for sale at Stanley's, a south-side neighborhood bar in Reading that had good reason to distribute it: Suds and Dregs gave Stanley's a 5B, or Five-Beer, rating, which is as high as they go. My purpose in buying the book was utilitarian. Like a lot of traveling people, I like to pause for a cold draught late in the afternoon, and I'm always happy to have the advice of any local who can warn me off the sort of joint where conversation is dominated by the host of "The Newlywed Game" or where, as Suds and Dregs once put it, the bartender has "the personality of a Handi-Wipe."

Leafing through *A Beer Drinker's Guide to the Bars of Reading*, I found that I liked the way Suds and Dregs approached the task at hand. The sentence or two they allowed themselves for summing up a place could be pointed ("It's like entering someone's living room — someone you don't know") or mysterious ("Pool table in back room. Nervous barmaid") or absolute ("We'll never go back"). The excuse for meeting Suds and Dregs that I finally came up with was prompted by a suggestion from a friend of mine that I take a look at an Allentown bar called Chick's Hotel Grand, which my friend described as the oldest stand-up bar in the country — the sort of solid, beer-drinkers' place that is increasingly hard to find now that so many taverns have redecorated into the sort of place Suds and Dregs have described as "disgustingly cocktail loungish." I figured I'd take Suds and Dregs along to Chick's as consultants. I also figured we might have a few beers together in Reading, just to put everything into perspective.

Reading is a beer-drinker's town. In John Updike's novels, it's the blue-collar town of Brewer, where Rabbit Angstrom and his fellow printers used to stop in a neighborhood bar regularly for a cold beer in the years before Rabbit fell in with that crowd of suburban Martini-sippers. Around the turn of the century, Reading's hosiery mills and railroad yards and packing plants drew Italian and Polish and German and Ukrainian workers who had a strong attachment to the local taverns that even now seem to be the only punctuation in block after block of row houses. The "Welcome to Reading" greeting I found in my motel room from Suds and Dregs was written, appropriately enough, on a brown paper bag. What was in the brown paper bag was even more appropriate. Naturally, there was a package of locally made pretzels — Bill Spannuth's Unique Pretzel Splits. The eighteenth-century settlers of Reading and the surrounding hills and farmland of Berks County were Pennsylvania Dutch — fortunately for Suds and Dregs, mostly Pennsylvania Dutch of the fancy rather than plain variety, so that they brought a taste for beer without the pietistic religion that would severely limit its consumption — and the entire area has always been known for its German pretzels. Until the middle seventies, when Reading decided to adopt a motto that would reflect the presence of dozens of factory-outlet stores in its abandoned mill buildings, it was known as the Pretzel Capital of the World.

My gift paper bag also contained a large package of Dieffenbach's Old Fashion Potato Chips, which are made not far from Reading, in Womelsdorf, Pennsylvania, in a small shed next to the Dieffenbach family's house, and which carry on the package in large letters the warning "Do Not Expose to Sunshine." I learned later that Suds and Dregs both consider Dieffenbach's to be the Best Potato Chips in Berks County — an encomium that embodies the collateral distinction of the Best Potato Chips in the World. Dregs once read somewhere that some potato chips made in Hawaii were the best potato chips in the world, but he later had the opportunity to taste the Hawaiian chips; he speaks of the experience in the tone of voice he normally reserves for discussing cocktail lounges that are decorated in flecked wallpaper and do a steady business in Singapore Slings. Dieffenbach's potato chips, it almost goes without saying, are cooked in pure lard.

Rummaging around further in my paper bag, I found a hunk of Lebanon bologna and a hunk of local cheese — both of which would be found on the plate of assorted cold cuts that a lot of Reading bars serve under the name of Dutch Platter. At the bottom of the bag were two bottles of Lord Chesterfield ale and two cans of Yuengling's Premium — products of Yuengling Brewery, in Pottsville, the oldest brewery in the United States and a place that Suds and Dregs visit regularly in the spirit that Elvis freaks visit Graceland. I spread the contents of the gift bag on the dresser — beer, pretzels, potato chips, bologna, cheese. A Reading banquet! I figured it would brighten up the hour or so I had to wait until Suds and Dregs arrived for a bar tour. They cannot start visiting bars until after three in the afternoon: both Suds and Dregs are high-school teachers.

Suds Kroge and Dregs Donnigan are *noms de bière*. The authors of *A Beer Drinker's Guide to the Bars of Reading* figured that the school authorities might not like the idea of Berks County youth being placed in the care of people whose sideline required attendance at places like the Anthracite Cafe and Stew's Keg and Dot Bilski's Tavern ("Decor: Hope Rescue Mission"). Suds and Dregs had started out with the intention not of writing a book but simply of visiting every bar in the city — a project that seemed to grow naturally from an effort to find a suitable meeting spot for an organization of beer drinkers that Suds and Dregs usually refer to as "the lodge." ("A bunch of white-collar teachers playing blue-collar for a night now and then.") As it happened, though, the guidebook made Suds and Dregs local celebrities, and the school authorities turned out to be tolerant, or maybe even a bit proud. I can see why they might be. Suds and Dregs, after all, set the students a good example of persistence and thoroughness. They did not miss one bar. Their efforts before the idea of a guidebook emerged could even have been seen as pure research. Also, they were ambitious. After the success of the Reading book, they expanded into the entire county — visiting 238 bars for *A Beer Drinker's Guide to the Bars of Berks*. They have been referred to by their real names in the local press with no ill effect. Suds is really David Wardrop. Dregs's real name is Bob Weirich. I call them Suds and Dregs.

ह्य

"This has it all," Suds said. "This is what it's all about."
We were at the Grand Central Tap Room, in Fleetwood, a town more or less on the way to Allentown.
In *The Bars of Berks*, the Grand Central got a 4½B
rating, and Suds and Dregs were at a loss to explain
what had led them to withhold that final half a beer
that would have indicated perfection. They like everything about the Grand Central. The clientele is what
Suds and Dregs tend to call "a good mix." Fleetwood
is a blue-collar town best known for having produced
the automobile bodies that gave the Fleetwood Cadillac
its name, but there is also a large grain elevator that
draws nearby farmers. Suds and Dregs dote on the
Grand Central's french fries, which are listed on the
menu board under Soups and Platters and which, it
almost goes without saying, are cooked in pure lard.
They love the decor — worn wooden floor, softball
trophies, a long bar with "pie-plate" bar stools, a
refrigerator for take-out six-packs with a television set
on top of it, a checkerboard on one of the tables, a display of potato chips and pretzels and lighter fluid and
razor blades and work gloves. They also like the priccs.
Suds and Dregs are conscious of what they always call
"value." Dregs was still boycotting a beer called Prior
Double Dark, because of a precipitous increase in its
price several years before. We were drinking half-
and-half — half Pabst draught and half Yuengling's
porter. Porter is a dark beer that, according to the
label on the bottle, is brewed by Yuengling "expressly
for Tavern and Family Trade." We were too early to

take advantage of an offer the Grand Central was making in honor of its centennial and reunion: after nine in the evening, three dollars bought a centennial beer glass that the management undertook to fill as often as necessary until eleven. Suds and Dregs believed the centennial offer to be particularly good value. "You get to keep the glass," Dregs reminded me.

We were at the Grand Central too early to take advantage of the centennial offer because Suds and Dregs had picked me up promptly after school, and we had headed nearly straight for Fleetwood — taking time only to have some draught Rolling Rocks at the Pricetown Hotel. Considering the amount of time Suds and Dregs have to spend in beer joints in the course of their research, they had struck me as remarkably trim and well spoken and neatly dressed — all in all, in fact, just the sort of young men to whose care you might be happy to entrust your high-school-age children. On the way to Pricetown, we had given a ride home to Suds's wife, Beth, who teaches home economics at the junior high next to the high school where Suds teaches graphics and printing and Dregs teaches English. I asked her if she had gone along to many of the bars being investigated for *A Beer Drinker's Guide to the Bars of Reading*.

"That was a different wife," Dregs said. "The first wife divorced him after the first book."

"Oh, that's a shame," I said, thinking partly, I'll admit, of the wasted dedication.

"I didn't think so," Beth said.

Suds had managed to hold on to his second wife straight through the research for *A Beer Drinker's Guide to the Bars of Berks,* although the suggestion that the dynamic duo follow up the county book by tackling the entire state of Pennsylvania did not fill her with enthusiasm. "Beth even guest-starred a number of times for the county book," Suds said proudly.

"Guest-starred?"

Someone who accompanies Suds and Dregs on their rounds, it was explained to me, is always referred to as a guest star. I was a guest star.

Because of a wrinkle in the liquor laws, a lot of Pennsylvania bars are called hotels, even though they often lack such hotel accoutrements as registration desks or lobbies or overnight guests. Chick's Hotel Grand turned out to be a corner bar that made a good first impression on both Suds and Dregs. "It looks like it has potential," Suds said as he walked up to the bar and ran his hand along a bar rail made of highly polished wood. Both the bar counter and the back bar — the shelves that bartenders normally use to display bottles of whiskey — were finely crafted of wood that had the look of decades of care. Under one end of the bar was a prize-fight bell that the bartender could clang any time someone bought a round for the house. One wall of Chick's was devoted almost entirely to pictures of Babe Ruth. Attention had also been paid to Carmen Basilio.

Suds and Dregs were impressed. They acknowledge a bias toward polished old wood and stamped-tin ceilings. Part of their interest in bars is obviously just an attachment to home ground. If they had lived in El Paso, I suspect, they would have done a book on every single Mexican restaurant in town, limiting their enthusiasm to the ones that serve menudo and allow only the mother of the family to preside over the kitchen. In Buffalo, they would be scholars of the chicken wing.

Suds and Dregs were less impressed by the Hotel Grand's clientele, two or three of whom looked as if a clang of the prizefight bell might find them unable to come out for the next round. One portly, gray-haired woman named Dorothy seemed particularly taken with Suds — she said he looked like a professor — and insisted on filling him in on what her life had been like in better days. She was drinking boilermakers. Just before we left, Dorothy pulled Suds aside for some intense conversation, and then started to weep — overcome with a sadness that seemed to have passed by the time we got to the door.

"A little too derelictish," Dregs said when we were back on the street.

"I'll say this for Dorothy," Suds said. "What started her crying was when she told me that a beer at the Hilton costs two dollars."

Dregs nodded in sympathy. "It's enough to drive anyone to tears," he said.

The next night, we finally got to Stanley's, a place Suds and Dregs revere as almost the model for 5B bars ("the kind of bars that make the world seem a whole lot better than it really is"). Stanley's appeal is not in the decor. A lot of brick buildings in Reading have glued-on facades of something called Perma-Stone — slabs of a dreary gray material whose appearance is made the more dispiriting by the implication in its name that it will be there forever. Stanley's has Perma-Stone on the *inside*. "At Stanley's, we rise above aesthetics," Suds told me. Although Stanley's is a Polish-run bar in a Polish neighborhood, its clientele is "a good mix," dominated by shift workers from a nearby box factory and meat-packing plant. The mix does not include women. Like a lot of Reading bars, Stanley's has what is still sometimes called a "side room" — a sort of family dining room accessible through a side entrance — and at Stanley's the side room has remained the only place where women and children are served. When Suds and Dregs drink at Stanley's, they tend to refer to their wives as "the little lady."

"One of the nice things about Stanley's is that if the little lady sends you out for groceries you can have a few beers at Stanley's and pick up some lunch meat and a dozen eggs before you leave," Suds told me. Although the barroom at Stanley's is small — there are maybe fifteen spots at the bar and three or four tables and a phone booth and a pinball machine — it seems to carry an inventory of goods comparable to a small K-Mart. Naturally, Stanley's has take-out six-packs and lighter fluid and potato chips and work gloves and lottery tickets. But it also has groceries and kerosene space heaters. On the back bar, among the bottles of rye and bourbon, there were signs that said "Genuine Antique Coin Necklace $4.00" and "Men's and Ladies' Watches $10.00" and "Gas-Teflon appliance connector $5.00" and "Picnic Table $10.00" and "Model Rolls-Royce $12.00." Suds and Dregs assume that Stanley, who was still behind the bar himself after forty or fifty years of owning the place, started selling model Rolls-Royces about the time he bought a full-size one for himself. Stanley's bar has always given good value — the draught prices listed on the back bar ranged from Piels at twenty cents to porter for thirty-five cents — and Suds and Dregs have concluded that the secret of Stanley's prosperity may be carried in the motto he once gave them: "I'd rather make a fast nickel than a slow dollar." In the side room, there was an entire table of for-sale items — men's jackets and "ladies' designer sweaters" and assorted vases and ceramic pigs and plates with pictures of Jesus Christ on them and boxes of banana-creme cookies. A sign over the table said, "Please Lord — Paralyze the Hand That Steals."

Suds and Dregs seemed to be settling in at Stanley's, and I was beginning to feel rather settled in myself. Stanley had made a lot of fast nickels on me, and before we arrived we had spent some time at Jimmy Kramer's Peanut Bar and a bar called the Shoboat Hotel — a place Suds and Dregs admire for its hunting trophies and always refer to as "the fur, fish, and game bar." I had come to believe that the evening was drawing to a close. Then Suds informed me that a friend of his from Berks Packing — a man who had just presented him with a ring bologna direct from the factory — had invited us back to the home of a colleague who was locally renowned for his homemade wine. That was going to put us behind schedule a bit, Dregs said, because we still had to go to the Paddock Bar and to a roadhouse in Reinholds, Pennsylvania, whose stamped-tin walls would knock me out. The evening, I realized, had just begun. The most bars Suds and Dregs ever visited in one evening while researching *A Beer Drinker's Guide to the Bars of Reading* was twenty-one. "And," Dregs said, "that was on a school night."

The Italian West Indies

I DAYDREAM OF the Italian West Indies. On bleak winter afternoons in New York, when the wind off the Hudson has driven Alice to seek the warmth she always draws from reading the brochures of ruinously expensive Caribbean resorts, I sometimes mumble out loud, "the Italian West Indies." Alice gets cold in the winter; I yearn for fettuccine all year round.

"There is no such thing as the Italian West Indies," Alice always says.

"I know, I know," I say, shaking my head in resignation. "I know."

But why? How did Italy manage to end up with no Caribbean islands at all? The French have islands. The Dutch have islands. Even the Danes had one for a while. The English have so many Caribbean islands that they have been hard put to instill in every single one of them the historic English gifts of parliamentary democracy and overcooked vegetables. The Italians have none. Christopher Columbus — a Genoan, as I remind my fellow citizens every year when Thanksgiving approaches, and the man who taught Ferdinand and Isabella how to twirl spaghetti around their forks — took the trouble to discover the Caribbean personally before the end of the fifteenth century. Try to get a decent plate of spaghetti there now. When I happen into one of those conversations about how easily history might have taken some other course (What if the Pope had allowed Henry VIII's divorce? What if Jefferson had decided that the price being asked for the Louisiana Purchase was ridiculous even considering the inflation in North American real estate?), I find myself with a single speculation: what if the Italians, by trading some part of Ethiopia where it's not safe to eat the lettuce, had emerged from the colonial era with one small Caribbean island?

I dream of that island. I am sitting in one of those simple Italian beach restaurants, and I happen to be eating fettuccine. Not always; sometimes I am eating spaghettini puttanesca. Alice and I are both having salads made with tomatoes and fresh basil and imported Italian olive oil and the local mozzarella. That's right — the local mozzarella. The sea below us is a clear blue. The hills above us are green with garlic plants. The chef is singing as he grills our fresh gamberos. The waiter has just asked us the question that sums up for me what I treasure about the Italian approach to drinking wine: "You won raid or whyut?" I say "whyut," and lean back to contemplate our good fortune in being together, soaking up sunshine and olive oil, on my favorite Caribbean island, Santo Prosciutto. "Ah, Santo Prosciutto . . ." I found myself saying out loud one brutal winter day.

"You know very well there is no Santo Prosciutto," Alice said.

"The English obviously had a lot more islands than they could use," I said. "Aren't they the ones who are always going on about fair play?"

"Why don't we go to Capri this spring?" Alice said.

Capri! I looked more carefully at what she was reading. It wasn't a brochure about a Caribbean resort. It was the atlas that William Edgett Smith, the man with the Naugahyde palate, had given us as a wedding gift. It's a boxed, lavishly illustrated atlas that probably set Smith back forty or fifty dollars and has cost me thousands. Smith is a world traveler himself. He once spent a year or so in India and, as far as I can gather, lived entirely on the steak sandwiches served in the coffee shop of the Akbar Hotel in New Delhi — the only unreconstructed meat-and-potatoes man on the subcontinent.

"Capri!" I said. I could think of some closer places to get a plate of pasta myself. The only warm one I really longed for, though — Santo Prosciutto, I.W.I. — obviously didn't exist. We have not always been successful in looking for a non-Italian Caribbean stand-in. Once, we spent a week or ten days on the French islands of St. Martin and St. Barthélemy, having heard

that they had become places where a tourist with a
serious interest in marine life could find himself a
serious bowl of bouillabaisse. As it happens, virtually
nothing edible is grown or raised on the islands of St.
Martin and St. Barts, meaning that the meat and
produce and, I suspect, a lot of the fish is brought in
from places like Miami and Puerto Rico — some of it
looking more in need of reviving than the accompany-
ing tourists do. It struck me at the time that the residents of Santo Prosciutto, descendants of peasants
who had managed to coax already-stuffed eggplants
from the cruel soil of Calabria, would scoff at the notion
of having to import tomatoes from Miami. We were
assured, though, that any number of imaginative chefs
had been drawn to St. Martin and St. Barts to accept
the challenge of running a French restaurant under
conditions that required liberating the lamb from
custom brokers in the San Juan airport. I realized after
a few bites of salad during a St. Martin dinner by the
sea that one of them must have been the woman who
used to run the cafeteria at Southwest High School in
Kansas City: I could recognize her touch with a grated
carrot anywhere.

I don't mean that we had nothing good to eat during
that trip. St. Martin has a noted resort called La
Samanna, where a couple can while away a few days in
casual luxury for the price of a smallish Steinway, and
the management gets around the ingredient problems
with gestures like flying in crawfish from Turkey. At
the Castelets Hotel on St. Barts, we had a sort of

nouvelle-cuisine eminence of marinated fish good enough to revive Alice's criticism of my policy of refusing to enter a nouvelle-cuisine restaurant without having taken the precaution of strapping a flask of heavy cream to my calf. There's no question that St. Barts is a charming island — I was particularly charmed by the soupe de poisson at a place called L'Entrepot — but I think I had been put off my feed a bit by a conversation that took place just before we had come over from St. Martin. I had asked a man who owns a restaurant for suggestions about eating on St. Barts — taking out my notebook to record his recommendations.

He considered my questions for a while. Then he said, "Stay away from the meat."

It was true that the trip we were planning for the spring was in celebration of Alice's birthday. It was true that we wanted to go someplace we had never been before — which ruled out Martinique, the one Caribbean island whose food almost led me to forgive the French for whatever chicanery they used to finagle it from its rightful Roman owners. But Capri? Capri was the sort of place that appeared in song titles. As it happens, though, Alice is a bit of a romantic — even if the romance entailed in a search for the world's best sausage has so far eluded her — and romantics actually like places that appear in song titles. Alice does not simply like Paris, she likes April in Paris. I think she is still itching to visit Capistrano, even though I once explained to her, after a trip there, that the swallows

return to the old mission on the same day every year
only in the sense that the Easter Bunny comes to our
house on a regular annual basis, and that a photograph
of the romantically historic old mission before "restora-
tion" shows it to be not easily distinguishable from a
low pile of stones. I suppose those observations
identify me as a nonromantic — someone whose reaction to seeing the sun set over some South Pacific
island is to wonder whether the local taxis have a sur-
charge for travel after dark, or whether the maid back
at the Tiki Harbor Inn routinely turns the bed light on
when she turns back the covers and therefore attracts
every mosquito between the hotel and Calcutta, or, most
often, whether the hotel dining room will have run out
of everything but the gray meat that was purchased in
large lots during the festivities surrounding an official
visit by the Duchess of Kent in 1957.

I suppose people who have a romantic in the house
should limit themselves to atlases in black and white.
Alice said that Capri was famous for its flowers and
views — an island so staggeringly beautiful that powerful people had built villas on its cliffs since the Caesars.
I said it was famous for its tour buses; a feature of
song-title sorts of places is the presence of hordes of
people who have heard the song. It occurred to me,
though, that we could do a lot worse than Capri. I had,
after all, suggested that for Alice's birthday we take a
trip of an extravagance appropriate to the occasion.
Even nonromantics like to make a grand gesture now
and then, preferably at off-season rates. Was I the sort

of husband who would start humming "Moon over Miami" simply because a no-frills fare to Florida might have gone back into effect? As Alice's birthday approached, was I going to search around for a revival of "Wish You Were Here" just on the chance that she might be inspired by "I'm Don José from Far Rockaway?" I made reservations for Capri.

ॐ

The other passengers on the hydrofoil from Naples had the look of the vaguely decadent European rich an American traveler might associate with Capri — sleek-looking Italians with Milanese money and Florentine luggage. The men wore white pants and espadrilles and had finely knit sweaters thrown over their shoulders. The women looked as if they spent half their time at Gucci and the other half in the gym. Did these folks eat pasta? They weren't the sort of people I have always envisioned sitting at the beachside cafe in Santo Prosciutto, picking at the gamberos with their fingers and knocking back the sort of local Italian white that goes down so easily that it could probably be consumed through intense osmosis. It occurred to me that, given the clientele, the restaurants on Capri might resemble those fancy Northern Italian places on the East Side of Manhattan where the captain has taken bilingual sneering lessons from the maître d' at the French joint down the street and the waiter, whose father was born in Palermo, would deny under torture that tomato sauce has ever touched his lips.

My concern on that point was eased when we settled in for lunch at a simple-looking place overlooking the beach. Spaghettini puttanesca was on the menu. Roasted eggplant and grilled shrimp were on the menu. So was a salad made of tomato, fresh basil, olive oil and mozzarella — a dish, it turns out, that is sometimes known as a Caprisian salad. The waiter approached us cheerfully and said, "You won raid or whyut?"

"I have to say this about Capri," I said to Alice after I had ordered a bottle of whyut, "the place has a certain amount of romance."

ॐ

I thought for a while that the ice cream in Capri might distract Alice from the views. Alice likes ice cream. A person who spent a lot of time, say, comparing the various chocolate ice creams available in lower Manhattan would not be described by Alice as a food crazy. I think it's fair to say that Alice's interest in ice cream cuts across national boundaries, but she makes a particular specialty of Italian gelati. Her discussions of Rome tend to dwell on a café in the Piazza Navonna whose tartuffo she finds sublime. When she is in a town that has a number of gelaterias, she can spend an evening going from place to place to inspect the merchandise, commenting from time to time on the richness of the vanilla or the smoothness of the hazelnut. Sometimes, she will announce, almost to herself, "I've come to a decision: I'm not having gelati inside a brioche this evening" — which still leaves the decision of what kind of gelati to have not inside a brioche.

The ice cream did not distract Alice from the views. In a place like Capri, Alice is still gazing out to sea long after I have become what I believe the German intellectuals call Viewsodden. I suppose a high tolerance for views goes along with being a romantic. In a restaurant with a view, Alice always wants to sit where she can see out the window and I am equally interested in facing the dining room — keeping my eye on the waiters on the chance they might pass by with something worth coveting. She likes views from cliffs and promontories. Like the late John Foster Dulles, I have been to the brink many times, always with Alice. On Capri, she managed to combine her interests by looking at the view while eating a hazelnut ice-cream cone.

"Look at the castle!" she said one day, pointing to a huge stone castle on a far-off cliff. We were in a cab on our way to a village called Anacapri, where, Alice had heard, a marvelous view of the Bay of Naples was available to anyone who happened to be willing to dangle in a chair lift run by someone whose face seemed familiar from an Alfred Hitchcock movie. Alice has always been fond of castles. She likes to imagine someone like the seventeenth Baron of Provolone presiding over the estate while the lady of the house — once just an ordinary girl from some place like Harrison, New York — is waited on by hordes of liveried servants, every one of whom addresses her as *Principessa*. As it happens, I always address Alice as *Principessa* myself while we're traveling in Italy; I find it improves the service.

"Gerber's baby food," the driver said.

Alice and I looked at each other, puzzled. The driver explained that the castle was owned by someone whose fortune derived from Gerber's baby food. It was perfectly possible, of course, that such a person could be married to a *principessa,* having won her, perhaps, with promises of unlimited puréed lima beans. Alice sighed. Romantic notions of the high life on Capri are not easily kept intact. That very morning, an article in a magazine in our hotel room — an article about the sort of chic, sophisticated fun that jet-setters have on Capri every night after the day-trippers go home — had been ruined for Alice by a paragraph that began, "For many years, Mr. Hornstein (the Puss 'n Boots cat food heir), who owned Villa Capricorn on Via Tragera, was considered the top party giver."

"Well, babies have to eat," I said, trying to cheer Alice up. "So do cats."

Alice, though, likes her castles inhabited by people whose source of wealth has long faded into the history of their ancient principalities. In a place like Capri, she is even more interested in castles built by people who were powerful so long ago that no trace of family remains — Caesar Augustus and the Emperor Tiberius and that crowd. One morning, as we were being taken around the island in a small boat, she seemed particularly captivated by a high stone wall that had been built up one of Capri's sheer cliffs and laced with

stairs that led to a huge villa at the top. It was the sort
of wall that could conjure up in the mind of a song-
title sort of person the picture of hundreds of North
African slaves laboring to please the haughty but
exceedingly tasteful Caesar who had chosen the most
difficult perch on the island for the summer residence
of his favorite concubine. Just then, the boatman turned
down the motor and came back to where we were
sitting. "Estair Villy-yoom," he said.

"What?"

"Estair Villy-yoom," he repeated. When I continued
to look puzzled, he pointed to the villa above the stone
wall and went into an imitation of somebody doing the
backstroke.

"Esther Williams," I said. "He says that villa belongs
to Esther Williams."

"But not the wall," Alice said. "She didn't build the
wall."

The boatman nodded his head knowingly. "Estair
Villy-yoom," he said. "All Estair Villy-yoom."

કે

When the cold wind began to blow the next winter, I
tried to be realistic about the Caribbean. "How about
Martinique?" I said to Alice. After all, we had liked
Martinique. It not only has local ingredients but a lot
of people who understand what to do with them —
French Creole cooks who know that sea urchins were
not put in the ocean merely to be stepped on. It even

has some views, although when we were there I was too busy stuffing down stuffed crabs to spend much time looking at them.

"Too bad there's no gelati there," Alice said.

"Well, that would require an Italian island," I said. "Some place like Santo Prosciutto."

"A little gelateria right in the piazza of the village," Alice said. "Specialists in hazelnut, although they would also do that chocolate-hazelnut combination. Nobody on a French island could understand about that chocolate-hazelnut combination."

"Ah, Santo Prosciutto," I said.

"Yes," Alice said. "Santo Prosciutto."

"Also, Alice, I was thinking," I said. "It would probably be the sort of place that couldn't really be harmed by being in a song title. Maybe something like 'A Plate of Pasta on Santo Prosciutto with You.'"

Noble Experiment

WHEN I HEARD that Lum Ellis was trying to put the entire city of Natchitoches,
Louisiana, on the Pritikin Diet, I knew he
was going to have his hands full. Any researcher of my
interests, of course, would have had a sort of perverse
curiosity about what Ellis was up to — the sort of
curiosity that an historian who always specialized in
military campaigns might have about a project to
study the origins of pacifism. I thought I'd better go
to Louisiana for a firsthand look, and Alice, to my
surprise, seemed to agree. She may have been harboring the long-shot hope that, like some hard-nosed
reporter who is sent to expose a cult of snake handlers
and becomes a convert, I might find after three or four
days with the Pritikin forces that I had an untapped
obsession for Grape-Nuts and mung beans. I must
admit that I was also drawn to Natchitoches by what
researchers call a collateral field of inquiry. To many

people, Natchitoches, a parish seat seventy miles south
of Shreveport, was always known mainly as the oldest
settlement in the Louisiana Purchase — a peaceful,
rather charming old river town where a lot of people
who live in nineteenth-century houses can tell you
precisely the year their house was built and how many
generations of their family have lived in it. To me, it
was always known mainly as the home of the Natchitoches meat pie.

In 1979, Edwin Edwards, who was then the governor
of Louisiana, announced that the state would contribute
forty thousand dollars toward an attempt to educate
the citizens of one Louisiana town in the benefits of
the high-fiber, low-fat diet advocated by Nathan
Pritikin, whose Longevity Center in California is so
expensive that it attracts the sort of people who are
friendly with the governor of Louisiana. Edwards said
he had chosen Natchitoches (pronounced, more or less,
"NACK-i-tish") partly because it is a microcosm of the
population of the state. It is true that in northern
Louisiana, an area whose culture sometimes seems
defined by a devotion to chicken-fried steak and a dread
of the Pope, Natchitoches is a town where people are
not shocked by exposure to either Roman Catholics or
cayenne pepper — a northern-Louisiana town with
some southern-Louisiana overtones. Although Natchitoches's celebration of its early French and Spanish
settlers concentrates on their houses rather than their
food, modern residents do eat, in addition to their
share of chicken-fried steak, some food that a lot of

people in northern Louisiana would consider foreign and maybe wicked — spicy meat pies, for instance, and dirty rice, and hot tamales, and even an occasional gumbo. Edwards — who, despite his Anglo name, is a Cajun from southern Louisiana — said that Pritikin would have found it easier to convert people in "other parts of the country where the food is no good anyway." On the other hand, he acknowledged that attempting such a project in Cajun country, where people's main interest in an old building tends to be what sort of food might be served in it, would be "too much of a test." I can still brighten up a gray winter afternoon by picturing the scene of Nathan Pritikin trying to explain his diet plans for Opelousas to the law firm of Sandoz, Sandoz & Schiff.

At the kick-off banquet for the Natchitoches project, held in the Student Union of Northwestern State University, Edwards, apparently attempting to reconcile his role as the host and his reputation as an unreconstructed Cajun, was quoted as saying, "A Cajun raised on gumbo and crawfish would just as soon die ten years earlier as eat this stuff, but it's a noble experiment." Lum Ellis thought that was an unfortunate remark, although not as unfortunate as a comment by one diner that seemed to make all the wire-service stories — the comment that the broccoli bisque, prepared with Pritikin-approved ingredients, tasted like "boiled cigarettes." Right from the start, Lum Ellis knew very well that he was going to have his hands full.

Those of us who struggle valiantly against the perils

of cynicism find ourselves sorely tested by a project
that uses state money in Louisiana to demonstrate a
health theory developed in Southern California. My
view of any project in Louisiana has been formed partly
by a conversation in New Orleans some years ago in
which a man I know in the French Quarter listened to
several people theorize about how the Louisiana Superdome might affect the tone and the economy and the
morale of the city, and then said, "What you have to
understand about the Superdome is that after the
financing the rest is commentary." According to one
school of thought in Louisiana, the only significant
question to ask about any state project is "Who's
writing the insurance?"

Even though he has been caught wearing a necktie,
Nathan Pritikin, who claims that he can reverse
cardiovascular disease through diet and exercise, has
many of the other characteristics associated with what
students of the Free-lance Cure might categorize as the
Southern California School — no formal training in
the field, cure claims that are questioned by the medical
establishment, a horde of satisfied and sometimes even
zealous customers, and a book that has been on the
best-seller list in both hardback and paper. Of course,
it is always possible, I have to keep reminding myself,
that when the Deity finally decides to reveal The Truth
to the human race — not simply the truth about what
sort of food we should eat but The Truth — He may
choose as His messenger a Southern-California health
guru who has a how-to book in the top ten and has

managed to recruit both John Travolta and Barbra Streisand as disciples. It has been written, after all, that God works in strange and mysterious ways. If He wanted to tell The Truth, why would he be so obvious as to put it in the mouth of a Nobel Prize-winning Harvard biochemist and father of four? The man from California would say, without qualification, that he had The Truth ("Really, Merv, I'm not putting you on — this is The Truth"), and the cynics would all say, very slowly, "Uh-huh, I'll bet, sure, right." Perhaps the messenger would decide to demonstrate The Truth through a state-government-funded project in Louisiana. The insurance would be handled through open competitive bidding. I tried to keep that possibility in mind when I went down to Natchitoches to see how Lum Ellis was getting along on his project — Project LIFE, as he had decided to call it — and try a meat pie or two, as long as I was in the area.

Lum Ellis is a sociologist, but saying that doesn't describe him, even if you know that he was once the president of the Natchitoches Chamber of Commerce. In addition to running the Pritikin project, he and his wife — the co-director of Project LIFE — were running a tour business on the side. He drove a Lincoln Continental. At one time, Ellis was a Baptist minister in Jonesboro — the sort of Baptist minister who was also named Jonesboro's Young Man of the Year. For a while, he was the host of a radio talk show in Natchitoches. While working as an assistant to the president of Northwestern State University, he ran, unsuccessfully, for state superintendent of education. By the time the campaign was over, the president he had assisted for eight years had moved on. Lum Ellis was faced with going back to the classroom — a prospect that didn't strike him the way it might strike, say, Mr. Chips. Along came Project LIFE — a one-year project with forty thousand dollars of state money and some more from the Pritikin Research Foundation. It beat Introduction to Sociology 104.

When Ellis spoke of his involvement with Project LIFE, he reminded me of a familiar character in old Hollywood movies — the male lead who tries to make the heiress understand that even though it's true he was secretly hired by her parents to bring some romance into her life before she succumbed to the rare and fatal illness, he had grown to love her truly. Not many months before I met him, Lum Ellis had known nothing about the Pritikin Diet except that the project to bring it to Natchitoches needed a director. The first time he saw Pritikin, he was unimpressed: the founder was wearing sandals with socks and carrying a small bag of fruit, and Lum Ellis thought he looked like "a German refugee." But eventually, Ellis told me, he became "a lead-pipe believer." He lost weight. He announced that he was through with salt and fats forever. ("I wouldn't mess up the taste of grits or corn with salt and butter.") He told me that the only contact he maintained with his former way of eating was an occasional burst of "intelligent sinning" — a Baptist preacher's way of describing a system that my friend Fats Goldberg, the New York pizza baron, calls "controlled cheating."

In Natchitoches, Ellis, as affable and chatty as any old talk-show host who had also been a preacher and a Chamber of Commerce president, played the role of the cheerful missionary — a "Hiya, honey" here and a "How ya doin', darlin'?" there, a cable-television show on the benefits of making gravy with cornstarch and making milkshakes with dry skim milk, a Project LIFE column every week in the *Natchitoches Times* ("It's sure good to be home . . . where we can make our fat-free strawberry milkshake in our blender"), a sprinkling of diet-cooking classes and exercise rallies and Happy Heart Month programs, an occasional expression of good-humored exasperation at the daunting task he had taken on ("They say they want to eat something that sticks to their ribs. You know what that means? Hard to digest").

"Sometimes," Ellis told me, "people come up to me and say, 'Lum, I ate an egg this morning and damned if I didn't think of you and feel guilty.'" Sometimes someone who was asked if he was eating a lot of fiber replied, as the director of the cable-television show replied one night, "I eat anything that doesn't eat me." For a while, there was some talk that as many as a couple of thousand of the sixteen thousand people in Natchitoches might be following the strict regimen of the Pritikin Diet, but after a time even Ellis didn't claim that many people in Natchitoches were lead-pipe believers — willing, say, to follow his example of carrying along Grape-Nuts and dry skim milk and a bowl and a spoon on business trips in order to avoid having to eat a sinful breakfast. What he did claim was that a significant number of Natchitoches residents — more than a third, according to a survey he had taken — had been led to change their eating habits in some way by the program. The survey was part of the research component of Project LIFE, the announced idea being to test the death and illness rates in Natchitoches during the year of the study against a control city. Although Ellis sometimes described Project LIFE as a "multiple-risk intervention study," he did not claim that its methodology was ever likely to be studied by public-health schools as a model. "In a little old project like this, we can't draw definite conclusions," he told one interviewer, in one of his rare understatements, "but we can add to the general body of knowledge."

While I was in Natchitoches, I went to a Kiwanis luncheon, and some of the Kiwanians, speaking from behind small mountains of food they had collected at the Holiday Inn buffet table (Salisbury steak, liver with onions, shrimp creole, rice, broccoli with cheese sauce, candied yams, black-eyed peas, bread pudding), told me that a lot of people in Natchitoches had cut down on salt and sugar. A manager at one supermarket said that people might have been asking for slightly leaner cuts of meat, although the demand for chopped pork to make meat pies had not been affected. The manager of Brookshire's Supermarket, a large man named Lonnie Casey, told me that the store was selling a bit more whole-wheat flour and an occasional package of Pritikin-approved sapsago cheese — the cheese Casey had been referring to a few months before when he told a visiting reporter from Houston, "God, I couldn't swallow that mess."

Brookshire's Supermarket was also baking a special Pritikin bread, and selling about a hundred loaves of it a week. "Do you eat it yourself?" I asked the man who baked it.

"Nope," he said.

"Have you ever tasted it?"

"Yes."

"What does it taste like?"

"Cardboard."

I took a bite. Cardboard with a slight aftertaste. It occurred to me that if Lum Ellis was willing to make a steady diet out of such things in the name of research he was a true man of science, Lincoln Continental or no Lincoln Continental.

Although one doctor in Natchitoches criticized Project LIFE on both medical and ethical grounds — he called it a publicly funded advertising campaign that happened to be advertising a diet that might not even be advisable for the general population — most people seemed to approve of any effort that called attention to the need for exercise and nutrition, even if they expressed that approval between bites of pork cutlet with gravy. The claims of Nathan Pritikin for his longevity clinic aside, after all, the belief that Americans would do well to heed his advice about cutting down on salt and sugar and meat is widespread — although not so widespread as to include the members of the Natchitoches Parish Cattlemen's Association. They went to Baton Rouge to try to block Lum Ellis's appropriation. What was worrying Ed Hunter, the president of the association, was that the Pritikin forces would figure out a way to dredge up from the murky statistics some way to confirm their diet's wonders, even though Hunter told me he was convinced that "if you shook all the bushes here hard you couldn't find a hundred people on that diet." In Hunter's view, Project LIFE was just an ad campaign that the citizens of Louisiana, including the beef farmers, were paying for. "It's going to benefit nobody but Nathan Pritikin," he told me. I pointed out that there was one other certain winner — James Lasyone, the proprietor of Lasyone's Meat Pie Kitchen & Restaurant.

Lasyone turned out to be a rotund, enthusiastic man who works in the kitchen of his place rather than in the dining room. After twenty-five years as a butcher in a Natchitoches grocery store, he began in the early seventies to see if he could start a commercial enterprise based on the meat pie that people in Natchitoches have always eaten at home. A Natchitoches meat pie is a half-moon pastry that has been filled with chopped pork and chopped beef and spices and then fried in deep fat — emerging as something close to an empanada. When there is a festival in Natchitoches — the annual Christmas-light celebration, say, or the old-home tour — meat pies are sold from stands. When there is a party, the hostess often orders them from one of the women around town known for the specialty. Years ago, a book on Natchitoches recalls, they were sold on the street by black children, who chanted "Hot-ta-meat pies. Red-d-d hot!"

Lasyone sold meat pies from his butcher counter for a couple of years and then opened up a restaurant next door with meat pies as the premier dish — served with a generous portion of dirty rice. Several years after the restaurant opened, a writer from *House Beautiful,* apparently in town to admire the old houses and the brick street that runs along the river, happened into Lasyone's, and the result was an article that Lasyone came to think of as "the break of a lifetime." Lasyone's began to show up in restaurant guides. Eventually, the tourists who came to Natchitoches Parish were looking not just for plantation houses but for a genuine Natchitoches meat pie. A meat-pie recipe was included with the brochure on historic sites. After a while, it became common to see a huge tour bus parked in front of Lasyone's Meat Pie Kitchen & Restaurant.

If Nathan Pritikin wanted to distribute a list of foods to be avoided at all cost, he could simply hand out the menu of Lasyone's Meat Pie Kitchen & Restaurant. Lasyone's daily special is likely to be something like smothered calves' liver. His dessert specialty is Cane River Cream Pie — a sort of cake with vanilla filling, chocolate syrup, and whipped topping. Lasyone does have vegetables, but when he serves okra he takes the trouble to fry it.

When Project LIFE began, Lasyone was somewhat concerned that tourists might get the idea he had switched from meat pies to mung beans and the sort of cheese that just about did in Lonnie Casey at Brookshire's Supermarket. Lasyone's concern had been provoked by a phone call from the American Express Travel Service asking about his involvement with the Pritikin Diet. "I told them I had nothing to do with it," he told me, "and then they booked two buses."

As it turned out, of course, Project LIFE worked to Lasyone's advantage. How could a television crew assigned to poke around in the eating habits of Natchitoches resist a cheery antithesis to the Pritikin thesis? Lasyone's Meat Pie Kitchen & Restaurant became more famous than ever. Lasyone told me that the year of Project LIFE was the best year his restaurant ever had.

Even Lasyone was quick to say that he has nothing against people trying to eat healthy food — although he does believe that efforts to change people's eating habits are doomed to failure. When the subject came up, he tended to look serious and responsible. "Lum Ellis is a fine fellow," he told me. "He's trying to make a living trying to get people on a diet, and I'm trying to make a living trying to get them off." He went on to explain how he makes the roux for the beef stew whose gravy he pours over the chicken-fried steak. "The only way to make a good roux is to start with pure hog lard," he said.

"Just the sort of thing Mr. Pritikin goes for," I said.

James Lasyone began to giggle.

A Stag Oyster Eat
Below the Canal

I BECAME AWARE of the Georgetown Volunteer
Fire Company's annual stag oyster eat and dance
while reading the premier issue of *Shellfish
Digest*. I try to keep up with the scholarly journals.
All-male dancing under the auspices of volunteer firemen was a new subject for me altogether, but then I
could say that about a lot of what was in that first
issue. What I took to be the lead article discussed the
Quik Pik, a machine developed by the Sea Savory Company to shake the meat right out of crab bodies. The
fragile-looking body of a Maryland blue crab is quite
capable of withstanding the sort of treatment the Quik
Pik deals out, the article reported, unless the shell is
already damaged — in which case the crab flies apart
as if it had exploded. ("However, these fragments can
be easily discarded.") The process requires such fero-

cious shaking that the first models of the machine lumbered right across the floor. When I feel myself in need of cheer and I can't seem to conjure up the picture of Nathan Pritikin presenting his diet plans to the law firm of Sandoz, Sandoz & Schiff, I try to imagine a couple of crab pickers being pursued across the shed by an aroused Quik Pik.

I had picked up the first issue of *Shellfish Digest* — which was then called *Shellfish News* and also appeared in the form of a newsletter called *Chowder* and eventually, like a crab growing a hard shell, evolved into a series of books on shellfish — while I was still under the illusion that all oyster knives were pretty much alike; none of them, after all, have any purpose beyond opening oysters. That issue, though, discussed at least sixteen different models, all of which it offered for sale. As one of those rare publications that combined elements of the literary magazine and the mail-order catalogue, the *Shellfish Digest* offered its readers the opportunity to send in for almost anything it wrote about — not including the Quik Pik, which weighs fifteen thousand pounds. Someone who thought he had simply ordered a mussel cookbook by mail could pick up *Shellfish Digest* and discover that he had actually written a letter to the editor. "Enclosed — my check and order for two knives and a subscription" was not an unusual beginning for a contribution to the *Shellfish Digest* letters column, and neither was "Very interesting magazine — please do not print order blank on reverse side of drawing." (Once, as it happens, an entire issue of *Chowder* was printed on the back of a placemat.) The editor's own book, *The Craft of Dismantling a Crab* — one edition of which he had the foresight to publish on stain-resistant paper — was offered for sale in that first issue, as was the clam knife described in a piece he wrote called "Editor Designs Sharp Dagger and Lives to Tell About It."

The editor, Robert H. Robinson, had by then sold some fourteen thousand copies of *The Craft of Dismantling a Crab*, which, being crustaceously ecumenical, also offers illustrated advice on dismantling clams, lobsters, mussels, oysters, and even whelks: "Discard the orange viscera (A) and the horny black operculum (B), which is like a trapdoor." I learned the sales figures while Robinson was taking me for a sightseeing tour of Georgetown — a pretty town of two thousand people which serves as the county seat of Sussex County, Delaware. I was there for the annual Georgetown Volunteer Fire Company Oyster Eat.

Sussex County is what people in Delaware sometimes call "below the canal." The Chesapeake and Delaware Canal slices right across the top of the state from east to west; most of what is urban and industrial lies above it. Wilmington is above the canal. Above the canal, there are people who live right next to Pennsylvania or just across the river from New Jersey. Sussex is the southernmost and most rural of the state's three counties — culturally as well as geographically as far below the canal as you can get. It is well down the peninsula that below-the-canal Delaware shares with the Eastern Shore of Maryland and an unlikely detached tail of Virginia — a peninsula that has the Atlantic Ocean on the east and not many years ago was accessible from the south and west only by ferry. Below the canal, change comes slowly. While I was in Georgetown, one of the law firms was renovating an old building near the courthouse for its offices, and the local legal fraternity was of mixed opinion about whether the firm was taking some risk by installing some of its lawyers on the second floor. In Sussex County, lawyers have always been on the ground floor. I was informed of this situation by Robinson's wife, Battle Robinson, who happens to be a lawyer herself. "People will walk upstairs to see a dentist," she said. "But nobody's sure if they'll walk upstairs to see a lawyer."

On the second day after any important election, Georgetown still celebrates Return Day, as it has for at least a hundred and fifty years — bringing together the winning and losing politicians to shake hands, march together in a parade, and help consume an ox or two. For years, it was customary in some parts of Sussex County to mark the opening of the oyster season with Big Thursday celebrations, which included dancing right on the dock or on a dancing board made out of a barn door. It seems to have been a predominantly male form of dance. Describing one of the most famous dancers of the early part of the century, a county paper wrote in the thirties, "Even when he was seventy-five years old he could dance for two or three hours along with his son 'Matt,' who survives him and is known throughout lower Delaware for his power of endurance on a dancing board." The Big Thursday celebrations eventually died out, perhaps because there came a time when fewer places along the Sussex County shore could count on having a celebratory oyster catch. A man who wants to do some stomping on a board while a fiddle plays, though, can still count on one opportunity a year — the Georgetown Volunteer Fire Company Oyster Eat. For the price of admission — seven dollars the year I went — he also gets all the oysters and beer and egg-salad sandwiches and hard-boiled eggs he wants. And he doesn't have to worry about behaving the way his mother told him to behave when there are ladies present. When I arrived in Georgetown, Robinson informed me that the fire company had managed to maintain the tradition of the oyster eat for forty-four years — even though the previous year the oysters had to be hauled up from Louisiana.

Georgetown, which is eighteen miles from the ocean, is not a place where everyone eats oysters routinely. There may not be such a place. Oyster eating is not geographically predictable. I once met somebody whose eating memories of a childhood in Iowa are dominated by a barrel of oysters kept in the cellar. In New York, some friends of ours who are South Dakota expatriates annually have people in for a Christmas Eve feast of oyster stew as a reminder of their home state. I suspect that oysters have been a traditional dish in parts of the upper Midwest because, compared with other seafood, they tend to keep — although I remain skeptical of an old newspaper item quoted in *Shellfish Digest* about an oyster that was eighty-six years of age when it attacked a fish dealer's tomcat. ("The octogenarian clung to the cat's tail," the fish dealer was quoted as saying. "I never saw the cat or the oyster again.") They don't keep that well.

I don't remember any oysters in the part of the Midwest I grew up in, but I have been trying to make up for their absence ever since I left. Since I have publicly identified myself as the person who once nominated Mrs. Lisa Mosca, of Mosca's restaurant in Wagaman, Louisiana, for the Nobel Prize because of the perfection of her baked oysters, it almost goes without saying that I have a strong appreciation for the oyster. I like oysters on the half shell. I think the New Orleans oyster loaf is a concept so brilliant that I look forward to an extensive research project some day investigating its origins. I love oyster stew. When our South Dakota friends cancelled their Christmas Eve oyster-stew bash one year simply because they had an opportunity to go to Egypt, I was outraged; Alice had to restrain me from picketing their apartment building.

Even near the shore, though, there are a lot of people

who won't eat oysters. Battle Robinson, who ate oyster stew as a child in the interior of North Carolina, told me that she seemed to meet a lot of people in Georgetown who claim some sort of allergy when the subject of oysters comes up. Oysters, like the wicked witch in some fairy tales, are ugly inside and out. On the half shell, they are eaten alive. Plenty of the regulars at the Georgetown oyster eat can't imagine why anyone would eat an oyster. According to Robinson, a notoriously gullible member of the Georgetown Fire Company who does not happen to be an oyster eater was told once that a member who is widely known for his foolhardiness can, on occasion, eat an oyster through his nose. To a non-oyster eater, apparently, that did not sound much more unlikely than downing one in the conventional manner, and it is thought that the gullible fireman might have believed the story even without the deft touches of verisimilitude that went with it — that the oyster had to be small, of course, and that the eater had to leave off sauce "else he'd sneeze."

Robinson and I walked to the oyster eat from his house. He had furnished me with an oyster knife and an International Harvester baseball cap, in the manner of an English country gentleman handing his guest a walking stick before the evening's stroll. (He later sent me a photograph of the two of us in our oyster-eat costumes; on the bottom of it he had taped the caption

"You can either help these two continue their Vo-Tech education in fender repair or you can turn the page.") The oyster knife had been picked with some care in Robinson's office. Robinson runs a county weekly that was founded by his grandfather, but he seems to treat it as more or less of a sideline — the way I imagine Leo Braudy treats English literature when he's in the heat of one of his cheese-steak research projects. The office file drawers had titles like "Crabs" or "Shrimp."

"What I would recommend to you is this Virginia Breaker," Robinson had said, hefting a nasty-looking little knife.

"Well," I said.

"No, this Murphy Gulf would be good," he said, rummaging around in another box.

"The Murphy Gulf would be fine," I said, realizing that with fourteen or fifteen other oyster knives available for consideration we might never get to the oysters. My favorite oyster bar in New Orleans, the Acme, used to close early, and I think the disappointment of arriving there several times only to find the door locked may have left me with a permanent anxiety about missing out on oysters; it comes over me as the sun falls.

I had been impressed by the careful selection of knives, but I had not found it encouraging that just before we left for the oyster eat Battle Robinson served a full dinner. I can't imagine a hostess in Providence sending people along to a Squantum club clambake after serving them a full dinner. The oyster eat has a reputation for raucousness, and I was getting the impression that some residents of Georgetown did not think of it as a serious eating event. Also, in this era of liberation and sexual equality, I naturally felt a bit awkward that Robinson and I were in the position of pushing back from the table, thanking the little woman for dinner, and wandering off for a bit of jollity at the fire hall. When I mentioned this to the little woman in question, though, she seemed unconcerned — more or less as if I had taken it upon myself to apologize for the fact that males had a stranglehold on the outdoor jobs of the Sussex County Sanitation Department.

When we arrived at the fire hall — a huge one-story building constructed of cinder blocks and painted pale green — I realized that Robinson, wise in the ways of life below the canal, had provided me with the appropriate costume. I had never seen a greater variety of baseball caps. Within a few minutes, I noticed caps that advertised Adams Oil Company, Hitchens Bros. Construction, Delaware Blue Hens, West Virginia University Mountaineers, Perdue Chicken, Paramount Chicken, Sussex County Country Club, Valiant Plant Food, Milford Sure-Crop Fertilizer, Magnolia Volunteer Fire Department, Joy Dog Food, Tull's Farm & Home Center, Enforce Air Shocker, and Firemen Are Always in Heat. The floor of the fire hall was instep-deep in sawdust. The fire trucks had been removed for the evening. There were a couple of trash barrels around, but I took them to be tokens. Six or eight tables had been set up for oysters steamed in the shell — tables with holes in the middle for shells and with raised central shelves for condiments. The oyster eaters stood around the tables opening or eating or having a beer while they awaited new supplies. All of them had their own knives, and a lot of them wore gloves. ("Oysters are the hardest and riskiest of all shellfish to open," Robinson has written. "Still, style is very important. As in dismantling a lobster, you are rated by performance and you can easily lower your rating by slipping and sending the blade of your oyster knife through your hand.") In one corner, somebody opened and served raw oysters. In another part of the hall, egg-salad sandwiches and hard-boiled eggs were being handed out. There were hundreds of men in the fire hall, practically none of them without a glass of beer in his hand.

In one corner, next to a bandstand where a hard-bluegrass band was playing, eight sheets of plywood had been arranged in a square to form a dance floor. Half a dozen men were stomping away, with a crowd around them furnishing encouragement with yelps and whoops. There are sometimes people at the oyster eat who become sufficiently inspired by the good fellowship and the drink at hand to make an inexpert stab at a few jig steps late in the evening (I might be put in that category myself; Robinson had the wit to stay off the boards), but most of the dancing at the oyster eat is done by a small group of people who come there to dance. The dance they do is sometimes called "flat-footing." Sometimes it resembles a jig, or what people in Tennessee call "clog dancing" — with hands in the pockets or behind the back. Sometimes it requires some serious stomping on the plywood. Some of the dancers danced alone, but most of them faced partners. Most of them seemed to be people whose families had always danced. "The old man taught us boys. He's been flat-footin' since he was eleven or twelve years old," I was told by Lawrence Coverdale, a young machinist from Milford, who danced mainly with his brother Jim. "We were raised up on it." There aren't many flatfoot dancers left in Sussex County, but because a few families took the trouble to raise some up, a number of them are young. I suspect that the oyster eat is in no more danger of running out of dancers than it is of running out of oysters. If it does, it can just haul some up from Tennessee.

Among the rest of the crowd milling around the fire hall — farmers and politicians and car dealers and swampers and first-floor lawyers — the main activity seemed to be talking and drinking beer. In fact, late in the evening I realized that, with talking and watching the dancers and having a few beers and trying out a few jig steps, I had not put much time in with my Murphy Gulf. I was not surprised the next day when I heard someone at a secondhand store asked if he had been to the oyster eat and he said, "Naw, I quit drinking." Battle Robinson may be from North Carolina instead of below the canal, but she knows enough to give people dinner before they go to an oyster eat.

Hong Kong Dream

I CAN'T COUNT the number of hours I have spent in Chinatown dreaming of Hong Kong. The spell usually comes over me after dinner, as I stroll down Mott Street, ostensibly engaged in what passes for after-dinner conversations on those outings — a sort of post-game analysis of the stuffed bean curd, maybe, or some mild disagreement over whether the pan-fried flounder was really as good as last time. Alice is always there, and often the girls. Sometimes, William Edgett Smith, the man with the Naugahyde palate, is walking down Mott Street with us, pretending to be in a sulk because nobody would let him order egg foo-yung. We are usually walking toward the amusement arcade, on Mott Street near Bowery, where it is possible to finish off an evening in Chinatown by playing ticktacktoe with a live chicken. A bag of fortune cookies awaits anyone who beats the chicken, but, as far as I know, nobody ever has. The chicken gets to go first — a sign on the outside of the cage lights up "Bird's Turn" as soon as the coins are dropped — and that advantage seems to be enough to carry the day. Some people think the chicken always wins because it is being coached by a computer telling it where to peck by means of lightbulbs that can't quite be seen from the outside of the cage. Some people think the chicken always wins because it happens to be one smart chicken. Sometimes during that after-dinner stroll — when we are discussing the pan-fried flounder, or when our best ticktacktoe player is being wiped out by a chicken, or when Alice and I are negotiating with Abigail and Sarah over whether it would be appropriate to compensate for our failure to win the fortune cookies by asking the Häagen-Dazs store and the David's Cookies store next to it to join forces for a chocolate-chocolate-chip-ice-cream sand-wich on chocolate-chunk cookies, or when I drop in to the supermarket across from the arcade to replenish my supply of fried dried peas — I am often heard to murmur, "I'd really like to go to Hong Kong."

"Don't you mean China?" I'm sometimes asked, if there's someone along who hasn't been with us before when I say "I'd really like to go to Hong Kong" as I'm strolling down Mott Street.

No, not China. I'll admit that the coverage of those banquets thrown during Richard Nixon's first visit revived in me what had been a flagging interest in superpower relations. For those of us who spend a lot of our evenings on Mott Street discussing stuffed bean curd, it was difficult to look at pictures of Nixon sitting at the banquet table — sitting there with a look that suggested he was longing for a simple dish of cottage cheese at his desk or for dinner at one of those Southern California restaurants where salad with Green Goddess dressing is set before you with the menu — and restrain ourselves from thinking, "Why him?" The opening of China to tourists did present a temptation. In New York, there are people — some of them members of my own family — who find it odd that someone wants to eat four or five Chinese meals in a row; in China, I often remind them, there are a billion or so people who find nothing odd about it at all. Soon, though, reports began to drift back from Chinatown denizens who had visited the People's Republic, enduring tours of primary schools and irrigation projects just to get a crack at the restaurants: the non-Presidential food was disappointing. The Chinese, I was given to believe, had other priorities — getting on with the revolution and that sort of thing. Fine. I'd wait. Meanwhile, I dreamed of Hong Kong.

For years, while China-watchers gathered in Hong Kong to interpret and reinterpret every bit of news from Peking, I remained in New York — a Hong Kong-watcher. From thousands of miles away, I analyzed news from the colony in terms of how it might affect my vision. When there were reports that another few hundred thousand people had been permitted to leave China for Hong Kong, I could see gifted chefs from Shanghai and Peking and Chiu Chow and Hunan — people who had chafed for years at having to read

"The Little Red Book" when they wanted to be reading recipes — rushing over the border, ready to knock themselves out for the running dogs of Yankee imperialism. In Hong Kong, I figured, people who felt the need to skip from one cuisine to another at every meal, like a fickle debutante who can't permit herself to dance with the same boy twice in a row, could simply say something like, "We just had Cantonese last night; why don't we go to a Peking place for lunch?" When I read that the Chinese businessmen of Hong Kong had far outstripped the English bankers who once dominated the economy of the colony — partly because real estate, traditionally controlled by the Chinese, grew to be much more valuable than whatever business was conducted on it — I could envision managers of the most expensive dining spots gratefully crossing Yorkshire pudding off their menus and beginning to compete ferociously for the hottest refugee chef. (But would rising real-estate values force rents too high for restaurants that concentrated on food rather than on flashy surroundings? We Hong Kong-watchers had a seminar on that one, over salt-baked chicken and dried Chinese mushrooms with bean curd.) When I read of Hong Kong's importance to the People's Republic of China as a source of foreign exchange, I could envision the political détente of my dreams — ingredients from the heartland of Communist China flowing into a place where capitalistic Chinese eaters were only too happy to pay for them. When the turmoil of the Cultural Revolution spilled over into Hong Kong, reviving talk of how easily China could take over the colony, some Hong Kong-watchers thought the dream had been shattered, but I was not among them. "Can't you see?" I would say, during one of our dim-sum symposia. "Now they'll be eating like there's no tomorrow."

My dream of Hong Kong was not a criticism of Chinatown. I love Chinatown. I love the outdoor market that has grown up along Canal Street, and I love the food stores where I can't ever seem to get anyone to tell me what anything is in English. I'm even fond of the chicken who plays ticktacktoe; I've never been a sore loser. I count myself fortunate to live a bike ride away from a neighborhood that is always mentioned — along with Hong Kong and Taiwan and Tokyo — whenever serious eaters of Chinese food talk of the world's great concentrations of Chinese restaurants. Still, Hong Kong is always mentioned first. There are weekend mountain climbers who take great joy in hauling themselves around the Adirondacks, but they dream of Nepal. Eventually, if they're lucky, they get to Nepal. Eventually, I got to Hong Kong.

ॐ

We were sitting in a restaurant called Orchid Garden, in the Wanchai district, beginning our first meal in Hong Kong, and I had just sampled something called fish-brain soup. I was about to comment. Alice was looking a bit anxious. She was concerned, I think, that over the years I might have created a vision of Hong

Kong in my mind that could not be matched by the reality — like some harried businessman who finally arrives in what he has pictured as the remote, other-worldly peace of a Tahiti beach only to be hustled by a couple of hip beach-umbrella salesmen wearing "Souvenir of Fort Lauderdale" T-shirts. Even before we had a meal, she must have noticed my surprise at discovering that most of the other visitors in Hong Kong seemed to be there for purposes other than eating. That's the sort of thing that can put a visionary off his stride. How would the obsessed mountain climber feel if he arrived in Nepal after years of fantasizing about a clamber up the Himalayas, and found that most of the other tourists had come to observe the jute harvest? It appeared that just about everyone else had come to Hong Kong to shop. Hong Kong has dozens of vast shopping malls — floor after floor of shops run by cheerfully competitive merchants who knock off 10 percent at the hint of a frown and have never heard of sales tax. There are restaurants in some of the shopping malls, but most of the visitors seemed too busy shopping to eat. It was obvious that they would have come to Hong Kong even if it had been one of those British colonies where the natives have been taught to observe the queen's birthday by boiling brussels sprouts for an extra month. That very morning, in the lobby of a hotel, we had noticed a couple in late middle age suddenly drawing close to share some whispered intimacy in what Alice, the romantic, took to be a scene of enduring affection until one of the softly spoken phrases reached her ears — "customs declaration."

The sight of all those shoppers racing around, their shopping bags bulging and their minds feverish with schemes for flimflamming the customs man, had not really disturbed me. Hong Kong is the sort of place that can provide more than one vision. There must be people, for instance, who see it as a symbol of flat-out free enterprise prospering next to the cheerless regimentation of the world's largest Communist society, and there must be people who see it as a hideous example of capitalist materialism next to an inspiring land of collective sacrifice — although either vision would be blurred by a visit to the People's Republic department stores in Hong Kong, which accept American Express, Diners Club, Visa, and MasterCard. What can the struggle of the two great forces for the domination of the world mean if the Reds are on Diners? My own vision could be similarly blurred, Alice knew, if the fish-brain soup turned out to be only marginally superior to the bird's-nest soup or hot-and-sour soup routinely ladled out in Chinatown — the sort of first course that would be mentioned briefly on the after-dinner stroll as a lead-in to the subject of whether we should try the fried dumplings next time. I hadn't even bothered to claim to Alice that my principal interest in a trip to Hong Kong was the opportunity it presented to expand some research I had been doing on the varieties of scallion pancakes; she knew I was on a pilgrimage. I had another spoonful of fish-brain soup. "To quote Brigham Young, a man who never ate a shrimp," I said, " 'This is the place.' "

I'm tempted to say that I never doubted for a moment that it would be, but of course I had my doubts. Even before our first meal, though, my confidence was being shored up. Like so many other visitors, I had rushed out on my first morning to make a purchase — in my case a guide to Hong Kong restaurants — and I was rewarded by learning that the discussions in Hong Kong about what the colony's future will be after the British lease on the New Territories expires in 1997 are rivaled in intensity by the discussions about which restaurant serves the best Peking duck. My vision of Hong Kong was built on the belief that it would be not simply a place where the fish-brain soup dazzled but also a place where people took it for granted that a normal response to hearing a visitor ask "What's Macau like?" would be to offer an opinion on which Macanese restaurant offers the most succulent prawns — a place, in other words, where priorities had been established. Within a couple of days, I felt like a China-watcher who, after having spent years spinning out generalizations about China based on the flimsiest perusal of monitored radio broadcasts and fanciful refugee accounts, is finally permitted to make an extended visit to the mainland and finds, to his astonishment, that he was right all along.

At the precise moment that this feeling came over me we had just finished dinner at a businessmen's club called the Shanghai Fraternity Association. We had eaten smoked fish and drunken-chicken and something resembling bok choy and shark's fin soup and mixed vegetables and fried pork and river shrimp and Shanghai dumplings and a sort of sesame fritter. What I had to keep reminding myself was that we were consuming the Hong Kong version of club food. One of our dining companions, an ore trader of Shanghainese background, had spent part of his afternoon consulting with the club management about precisely what should be served. That, I was told, is routine among Hong Kong businessmen who entertain. I tried to imagine an English or an American businessman giving over part of his afternoon to planning a meal at his club. Even if it occurred to him to do it, what would he say? "Let's be sure to have some of those tasteless canned vegetables, Emile. And what sort of spongy gray meat is good this time of year? And a dinner salad of iceberg lettuce would be nice, I think. With Green Goddess dressing."

 howeverﾠ

It was the rain that drove me into the Central Market of Hong Kong. I stayed only a couple of minutes. I have a weakness for markets, but when it comes to Chinese food I have always operated under the policy that the less known about the preparation the better. Even in Chinatown, it seems to me, a wise diner who is invited to visit the kitchen replies by saying, as politely as possible, that he has a pressing engagement elsewhere. That policy of selective ignorance should obviously be followed in Hong Kong, where old hands are often heard to mutter, "The Cantonese will eat anything." What astounded me about the Central Market — in the short time I had for observation before I decided that I preferred the rain — was not simply that it was a place where a moderately energetic public-health inspector could write his year's quota of citations in fifteen or twenty minutes. I was even more amazed by the fact that, even though the same purveyors presumably operated out of the market routinely day after day, there was something impromptu about it. People squatted on the floor here and there, between a basket of squid and a couple of discarded cattle heads, as if they had merely wandered by to say hello to a fishmonger friend who said, "Listen, Joe, as long as you're here, why don't you just sit yourself down on the floor over there and peel this pile of shrimp?"

Even after I started giving the Central Market a wide berth, I found unwelcome knowledge creeping through my defenses. In Chinatown, for instance, I had always taken it for granted that the "bird's nest" in bird's-nest soup was a direct translation of some evocative Chinese phrase describing some sort of vegetable that grows only in certain districts of certain provinces. It wasn't until I wandered into some Hong Kong shops that specialize in selling them that I realized that a bird's nest is a bird's nest — a swallow's nest, to be exact, usually imported from Thailand. What did that say about fish-brain soup?

Whatever it was, I resolved not to listen to it. "It's all a matter of mind-set," I informed Alice. "What we're talking about here is a vision, a ceremony. A person taking Communion doesn't need to know where the wafers came from." Fortunately, the rain got worse; even strolling along Hong Kong streets became difficult. I suppose there were visitors to Hong Kong who fretted about being prevented from taking in the countryside of the New Territories and observing the culture of the inhabitants. The shoppers must have been irritated, considering how easily a sodden shopping bag can break through at the bottom. I remained cheerful. Between meals, I sat in the hotel room, going over lists of restaurants, protected from markets and shops — from everything but the final results.

᠊᠊᠊

Duck better than any duck I had tasted in Chinatown. Fried seaweed better than the fried seaweed we used to eat in Peking restaurants in London. Shad brought to the table sizzling on an iron plate. Yak fondue. Dim sum. More dim sum. Duck tongues (undoubtedly, I told myself, some colorful Chinese phrase for a particularly conventional cut of beef). Minced abalone and pork wrapped in lettuce leaves. I was reeling. I wondered what happened to some of those mountain climbers when they finally get to Nepal. Did they get up there on one Himalaya or another, in that thin air, and decide that they could never return to a place where mountain climbing meant schlepping to foothills on the weekend? Did they just stay in Nepal, eking out a living as consultants to the jute marketing board?

The question was in my mind one evening when we were having dinner in what appeared to be a rather ordinary Hong Kong restaurant — it was a last-minute substitution after the place my research had dredged up turned out to be closed — and noticed on the menu some of the same dishes served by one of our favorite restaurants in Chinatown. We ordered two of them — roast pigeon and fried fresh milk with crabmeat. The pigeon was a lot better than the Chinatown version. The fried fresh milk with crabmeat was so much better that it tasted like a different dish.

"We haven't tried the pepper and salty shrimp," Alice said.

We had both noticed it on the menu. As it happens, the Chinatown restaurant's finest dish — even better than the pigeon or the fried fresh milk with crabmeat — is by far the best version of pepper and salty shrimp I have ever eaten.

I thought about ordering pepper and salty shrimp. I suspected it would be better than the Chinatown version, but I wasn't sure I wanted to find out. The minced abalone and pork wrapped in lettuce leaves that we had eaten in Hong Kong was superior to the version we sometimes eat in a Chinatown restaurant, but something about finding that out had seemed almost disloyal: Abigail and I are so fond of the Chinatown version that our definition of a truly special treat is for the two of us to sneak down there on a school holiday and make a lunch out of however many orders of it are required to fill us up. I live only a bike ride away from Chinatown, after all. I miss it when I'm out of the city, even when I'm in Hong Kong. I miss the stroll down Mott Street toward the amusement arcade. I almost miss the chicken. It occurred to me that even people interested in knowledge for its own sake have to set some limits to how much they want to know.

"I think I'm kind of full," I said to Alice. "Maybe we should save it for next time."

Just Try It

WHAT I DECIDED to tell Sarah about cat-fish was that it tastes like flounder. She eats flounder, although I can't say she's an enthusiast. When it comes to food, her enthusiasm runs toward chocolate — her favorite dish (if that's the word) being a chocolate-chocolate-chip-ice-cream cone with chocolate sprinkles. She once went in the Village Halloween Parade as a chocolate-chocolate-chip-ice-cream cone with chocolate sprinkles — the ultimate tribute. I can't remember what I told her flounder tastes like. Whatever it was must have been mentioned in a speech of considerable eloquence. There is general agreement in our family that my speeches on how closely Chinese fried dumplings resemble ravioli were as persuasive as any I have delivered — Sarah happens to love ravioli; I wouldn't be at all surprised to see her suit up as a ravioli some Halloween — but four years of such speeches were required before Sarah agreed to take one microbite of one dumpling. Trying to persuade Sarah to taste something is not a struggle that is undertaken in the expectation that success will be rewarded with the opportunity to see her yelp with joy as she cleans her plate. She's not likely to be crazy about it. Once, Alice used a food processor and creamed cheese and absolutely fresh spinach and considerable imagination to turn out a spinach dish one bite of which would have probably caused Paul Bocuse and maybe even Herman Perrodin to ask about the possibility of apprenticing for a while in Alice's kitchen. Sarah tasted the spinach and, displaying a certain sensitivity toward the feelings of the chef, said, "It's better than a carrot." I must admit that the chef and I have found that phrase useful ever since. As we walk out of a movie, one of us sometimes says, "Well, it was better than a carrot" or, occasionally, "That one was not quite as good as a carrot."

The notion that Sarah might be persuaded to taste catfish was based on my observation that she might have been growing slightly more adventuresome about nonchocolate foodstuffs. The days are past when she refused to go to Chinatown unless she was carrying a bagel ("just in case"), and even though she still doesn't eat salad, she is too old to repeat her grand preschool gesture of refusing to return to a summer-recreation program because those in charge had the gall to serve her salad at snack time. Slowly, arbitrarily, she has expanded to half a dozen or so the exotic dishes she enjoys in apparent contradiction to her entire policy on eating — so that she will casually down, for instance, a Chinese dish called beef with baby clam sauce, like a teetotaler who happens to make an exception for slivovitz or south-Georgia busthead. Still, I often hear myself making the sort of appeal I can imagine thousands of parents making to thousands of ten-year-olds at the same time: "Just try it. Would I lie to you about something as important to me as fried dumplings? If you don't like it, you don't have to eat it. Just try it."

There are, of course, a lot of grown-ups who won't try catfish. Some people think catfish are ugly. To be perfectly honest about it, just about everybody thinks catfish are ugly. I have run into people willing to defend the looks of hyenas and wild boars, but I have never heard anyone say, "The catfish, in its own way, is really quite beautiful." A catfish has whiskers that might look all right if attached to some completely different animal — although an appropriate animal does not come immediately to mind. The best thing that can be said of a catfish's skin is that it is removed before eating. At a fish plant, anyone who cleans catfish is ordinarily called a catfish skinner; part of the process is to pull off the skin with the kind of pliers that are used by other people to snip the heads off roofing nails. People who are particularly conscious of the tendency of catfish to feed along muddy river bottoms think of cleaning a catfish as a process that has ultimate failure built right into it; they avoid catfish precisely because they believe that there is no such thing as a clean catfish. Some people avoid catfish because they believe that no catfish — even one whose bones have been removed by a boner with the skill of a surgeon — is harboring fewer than seven small bones somewhere within it. There are also people who wouldn't think of trying a fish that in some parts of the country is thought to be eaten mainly by poor folks. In the South, where most catfish is consumed, even the way restaurants customarily advertise it implies that they are offering a bargain rather than a delicacy — "CATFISH AND HUSHPUPPIES, ALL YOU CAN EAT: $3.25." Writing in the *New York Times* once about the place of catfish in his Mississippi boyhood, Craig Claiborne did describe the pleasure of eating it on summer picnics that included ladies carrying parasols, but he also left the impression that catfish was eaten on picnics because his mother wouldn't allow it inside her house.

With catfish farming now a considerable industry in Mississippi and Arkansas and Alabama, there has been some effort in recent years to make catfish a respectable national dish, rather than a slightly disreputable regional specialty, but seeing it on the menu of the sort of eclectic Manhattan restaurant that also serves salmon mousse and fettuccine with wild mushrooms still leaves the impression of having run into a stock-car racer at a croquet match. I preferred to think, of course, that the class implications of catfish eating would have no effect on Sarah's willingness to try it out — we have tried to raise her to believe that honest pan-fried chicken is in no way inferior to pâté — but it is impossible to predict such things; she happens to love particularly expensive cuts of smoked salmon, and the first wild-card dish she doted on in Chinatown was roast squab.

Naturally, I am interested in any opportunity to nudge Sarah's eating habits in a democratic direction, and that was one reason I chose the Fourth Annual St. Johns River Catfish Festival in Crescent City, Florida, as the destination for a little trip we were planning to take together while the rest of the family was occupied elsewhere. The other reason was that I happen to love catfish. I even love hushpuppies. Sarah was enthusiastic about going to Florida, although I must admit that the first question she asked was how far Crescent City is from Disney World. Then she narrowed her eyes and said, "Catfish?"

"It tastes like flounder," I said. "You can just try it."

"OK," she said, in the voice she uses for acknowledging the necessity of wearing gloves on cold days. "Maybe."

"Their other specialty is alligator tail," I said. "And for all I know alligator tail may taste like flounder, too."

Sarah didn't bother to reply to that one.

ৡ৶

"I might try some catfish," Sarah said on the day before the festival, as we were discussing preparations with its founder, Ronnie Hughes. "It depends on how it looks."

"If you don't have any before the catfish-skinning contest, I suspect you won't have any after," Hughes said.

It was clear by then that the people in Crescent City, a pleasant little north-Florida town below Jacksonville, were not among those trying to tidy up the reputation of the catfish. When Hughes, the publisher of the *Crescent City Courier-Journal* and *Trading Post Shopper*, persuaded the Rotary Club to sponsor a catfish festival, it was partly with the idea of celebrating the local commercial catfishing industry, but there has never been any claim that what the fishermen catch is anything other than an ugly beast with more bones than any fish has need of. "It's not something that's going to grace a table," Hughes said. Among the articles in his newspaper's Catfish Festival supplement was one that investigated the various styles of trying to eat a catfish — styles that divided catfish eaters into pickers, peelers, chompers, suckers, spitters, and animals — and concluded that all of them were more or less unsuccessful. In other parts of the South, boosters of the domestic catfish industry may argue for wider acceptance of their product on the ground that farm-raised catfish do not have a muddy taste; a resident of Crescent City tends to say he prefers the wild catfish caught in the nearby St. Johns River precisely because they do taste muddy. People around Crescent City take the catfish on its own terms.

"We don't mind if you refer to Crescent City and southern Putnam County as 'the sticks' or 'red-neck country,'" the brochure that the Rotary put out for the Catfish Festival said. "We're a down-home community." In north Florida, it is common to hear people speak of their part of the state as "the real Florida" — meaning that it is the part still not dominated by tourists or retired Yankees or Cubans or anybody else except people who like to refer to themselves as crackers. "This here's a natural Florida cracker here," is the way Buck Buckles, the man who always presides over the preparation of the festival's swamp cabbage, was introduced to Sarah and me. The celebration of crackers in southern Putnam County is for qualities pretty much like those attached to the catfish — being ornery and plain and uncouth and unconcerned about offending the pompous ("He don't care," Gamble Rogers, a country storyteller who performed at the festival, said of a cracker fisherman in one of his stories who rams the boats of tourists. "He flat do not care") and basically lovable.

Being down-home, people in Crescent City would not think of calling swamp cabbage by its other name — hearts of palm. They sometimes refer to another local specialty, shoft-shelled turtle, as "cooter." Buck Buckles, whose crew helps him gather four hundred Sabal palm trees every year from an area scheduled for clear-cutting, is aware that some people serve hearts of palm fresh in salad, but for the Catfish Festival he cooks swamp cabbage for a day or so with noodles and salted bacon.

"How did you happen to learn how to do all that?" I

asked Buckles, a friendly man in his sixties who has worked most of his life as a heavy-equipment contractor.

"Ever hear of Hoover?" Buckles said. There wasn't much money around southern Putnam County in the thirties, he told me, and anyone who wanted something to eat often had to "catch it, tree it, cut it out of a palm, or scratch it out of a hole."

Sarah was impressed with the process of preparing swamp cabbage — cutting the trunk of the palm into logs and then using machetes to strip away one layer after another in order to reach the heart. She announced, though, that she wasn't going to try any. I hadn't expected her to. The name "swamp cabbage" didn't seem to bother her, but she never eats anything that might ever be part of a salad — just to be on the safe side.

I also hadn't expected her to try the sort of exotic meats that Satsuma Gardens, a restaurant ten miles up the road from Crescent City, includes in what its menu lists as a "Swamp Critter Special" — frogs' legs, soft-shelled turtle, and gator tail. I was eager to taste gator tail myself — partly because it is the only exotic meat I have ever run across that nobody seems to describe as tasting like chicken. I suppose I harbored some faint hope that somebody might interest Sarah by saying that it tastes a bit like roast squab — as it turned out, most people in Putnam County compare gator tail to pork chops — but after we had a talk about alligators with John Norris, one of the proprietors of the St. Johns Crab Company, that hope evaporated. The St. Johns Crab Company is a few miles from Satsuma, in Welaka, where there are a number of fish plants that buy the crabs and catfish that the same families have been hauling out of the St. Johns for generations. The company provides a lot of the catfish eaten at the festival, although the impossibility of diverting four tons of small catfish — the kind Southerners like to eat — from regular customers once a year means that the festival supply is quietly supplemented by some farm-raised catfish from Mississippi, with the hope that festival-goers will not be able to detect that telltale lack of mud.

"They don't just take a whole alligator tail and serve it like that," Norris said, in a reassuring way. "They cut out the muscle —"

"Well," I said, in the tone of someone who has been reassured, "once they dispose of that, then —"

"That's the part you eat," Norris said.

As it turned out, I liked gator tail — at least the way it was prepared by Jack Ketter at the Satsuma Gardens, a friendly little roadside restaurant that is decorated with a beer-can collection and signs with sayings like "A Woman with Horse Sense Never Becomes a Nag." The first time I tasted alligator — at a vast, crowded restaurant where the meal reminded me once again that any time you're called to your table over a loudspeaker, what you are served there is likely to be disappointing — I found it rather, well, muscular. Ketter, though, serves a first-rate gator tail — cut into thin slices, pounded, and lightly fried. In fact, he caters the gator-tail booth at the festival, since alligator can be served only by a restaurant proprietor licensed to buy meat from the supply acquired by the shooting of "nuisance gators" that have been declared an exception to the alligator-protection law because of a tendency to frighten golfers or snack on Airedales. "It tastes like veal scallopini," I said to Sarah during our second meal at Satsuma Gardens. The remark did not inspire Sarah to pick up her fork for a taste. She doesn't eat veal scallopini.

"I might have tried alligator if that man hadn't told us about the muscle," she said, glancing at my dinner of alligator, catfish, soft-shell crab, fried mushrooms, fried okra, and coleslaw. As it was, she was having a hamburger — which is what she had eaten for lunch at Satsuma Gardens the previous day. "This place actually has very good hamburgers," she said. "In fact, excellent." At our first Satsuma Gardens meal, the waitress who brought Sarah a sack of potato chips as a side dish (if that's the word) opened the sack as she placed it on the table, and I, remembering that some particularly sophisticated people trace their worldliness to having been taken as children to restaurants by fathers who advised them on selecting the wine and dealing with the captain, looked at the open sack and said, "That's the way you can tell a classy joint."

ॐ

The Fourth Annual St. Johns River Catfish Festival was held in the Crescent City town park — a long, square block in an area dominated by huge live oaks with Spanish moss. Sarah liked it. She liked the arts-and-crafts booths, particularly the booth that displayed a talking parrot. She liked the parade, which featured a series of Shriners driving by in every conceivable sort of vehicle that a grown man could look silly driving. She was impressed by Geetsie Crosby, the lady who always presides over the catfish chowder at the festival: Mrs. Crosby told Sarah that her own daughter would eat nothing but canned tuna for most of her childhood, and managed to grow up to be a very fine doctor.

"Maybe one of these years we can find a canned-tuna festival," I said. I had the feeling that Sarah wasn't going to eat much catfish. She had seemed to be preparing me for that on the way to the festival when she said she wasn't really all that hungry. When lunchtime came, I got one catfish dinner instead of two, and offered her a bite.

"I don't really think I want any, thanks," Sarah said.

"But it tastes like flounder," I said.

"Does it taste like chocolate?" she said.

I didn't think I could make a very good case for its tasting like chocolate. I hadn't really expected the question. "Well, at least that leaves us free to go over and watch the catfish-skinning contest," I said. "As soon as I finish eating."